The POWER Series

America's
DRUG ENFORCEMENT
Air Force

Customs, Coast Guard, CAP, DEA and DoD Airborne Drug Busters

Nena Wiley

Motorbooks International
Publishers & Wholesalers

To the men and women of the Civil Air Patrol
who help fly the war against drugs
every day . . . across the United States,
Alaska, Hawaii and Puerto Rico.
To them, and to all the aircrews that
qualify as drug warriors—
Customs, Coast Guard,
Air Force, Air National Guard, Air Force Reserve,
Border Patrol, DEA, CIA and others—
I salute you!

First published in 1992 by Motorbooks International Publishers & Wholesalers, PO Box 2, 729 Prospect Avenue, Osceola, WI 54020 USA

© Nena Wiley, 1992

All rights reserved. With the exception of quoting brief passages for the purposes of review no part of this publication may be reproduced without prior written permission from the Publisher

Motorbooks International is a certified trademark, registered with the United States Patent Office

The information in this book is true and complete to the best of our knowledge. All recommendations are made without any guarantee on the part of the author or Publisher, who also disclaim any liability incurred in connection with the use of this data or specific details

We recognize that some words, model names and designations, for example, mentioned herein are the property of the trademark holder. We use them for identification purposes only. This is not an official publication

Motorbooks International books are also available at discounts in bulk quantity for industrial or sales-promotional use. For details write to Special Sales Manager at the Publisher's address

Library of Congress Cataloging-in-Publication Data
Wiley, Nena.
    America's drug enforcement air force /
      Nena Wiley. p. cm.—(The Power series)
    Includes index.
    ISBN 0-87938-573-1
    1. Aeronautics in police work—United
States. 2. Narcotics, Control of—United
States. I. Title.   II. Series: Power series
(Osceola, Wis.).
HV8080.A3W55 1992
363.4'0973—dc20   91-39367

On the front cover: *A US Customs Black Hawk and crew hovering overhead means certain arrest to drug smugglers.* Scott Thode, JB Pictures

On the back cover: *Top left, US Coast Guard helicopters, airplanes and crews are powerful assets in the fight against drug smugglers* (USCG). *Top right, airborne drug smugglers are now up against the latest jet fighters, such as this Air National Guard F-16* (Florida Air National Guard). *Below, the patch worn by the high endurance drug trackers of Customs' Miami Air Branch.*

On the frontispiece: *Seventeen marijuana leaves painted on the fuselage of a US Customs Falcon attest to seventeen doper busts.* USCG

On the title page: *Customs Black Hawks await their next mission.*

Printed and bound in Hong Kong

Contents

Acknowledgments

This project would not have been possible without the support, patience and encouragement of my husband, Mike, and my children, Michael, Marta, Crissi and Sammy. Their love, respect and understanding allowed me time and space, countless days and nights away from home on field research to fly with the good guys while they wondered if I was ever coming home, and quiet dawns with the mockingbirds to sing my own literary songs.

I also wish to express my appreciation to NORAD, to the US Coast Guard and to the aircrews of the Air National Guard and Air Force Reserve for their support and candid briefings regarding Department of Defense counternarcotics operations.

I would also like to acknowledge the photographers who allowed me to use their photos for this book, in particular Scott Thode and JB Pictures, New York.

A special thanks to Mayra and Lt. Col. (Ret.) Robert "Cass" Cassaro. Mayra, for her never-ending provision of fresh, hot, strong coffee and Cass for his Machiavellian red pen.

Finally, much of the credit for this book must go to US Customs folks at CNAC, C3I West and the Public Affairs Offices, Branches and Aviation Units of the Customs Service. In particular, the Miami Aviation Branch with whom I did my most serious research over the past five years. The philosophy, assistance, suggestions, explanations, hands-on opportunities, experiences and good-natured ribbing provided by the Miami Customs warriors was singular! It is with honor and pride that I wear the "DW" patch. If this book gets by them, I'll be content.

Glossary of Air Intercept Terms

Angels: Reference to aircraft altitude in thousands of feet

Bandit: Hostile target

Bingo: Minimum fuel required to return to base

Bogey: Unidentified target

Bogey Dope: I need information on an unidentified target

Boresight: To align a sensor with a known axis (fuselage) or to align two sensors to a common axis

Break Lock: To lose the automatic radar tracking capability of a target

Close Trail: Two or more aircraft staggered one right behind the other

Closure: Relative closing velocity between two aircraft

Contact: I have raw radar return (skin paint) on a target

Copy: I acknowledge your message

Feet Dry: Aircraft is over land

Feet Wet: Aircraft is over water

Hard Left/Right: Normally used to direct a moderate-intensity turn (designed as a defensive reaction)

Judy: I will take control of an intercept (no more assistance is needed)

Lead: To position an interceptor in such a manner that the aircraft's nose remains pointed ahead of a target's flight path (on a collision course)

Lock-On: I have automatic radar tracking capability on the target

Max (performance): The greatest possible aircraft performance for the existing state of thrust and airspeed

No Joy: I have negative radar or visual contact with the bogey

Paint: I have an IFF radar return display on the scope from a target of interest

Position: Used to ascertain location of a friendly aircraft when visual confirmation is unavailable

Roger: I understand

RTB: Return to base

Sort: To distinguish friendly aircraft from suspect or known hostile aircraft

Tally-Ho: I see the bogey

Tracking: The act of locking a radar or infrared sensor onto a target

Visual: To confirm sight of a friendly aircraft

Wilco: I will comply

Part I—Customs Warriors

Chapter 1

Let's Go Hunting!

The Scramble
Homestead Air Force Base, Florida,
1845 local
The loudspeaker, broadcasting into the Customs ready room, shatters the complacency of its inhabitants.

"Scramble the Citation! Scramble the Citation!"

Four people are jolted to their feet. They grab their gear, swing open the door and run toward the ramp where the alert bird stands ready. They are the pilot, copilot, Air Intercept Officer (AIO) and the author.

The pilot makes a quick detour to the operations desk for mission data while the rest of the crew strap into the aircraft for immediate launch. The pilot jumps in, pushes the start button and also straps in. The APU (auxiliary power unit) is unplugged by ground crews, the chocks are pulled and the aircraft is under way as the second engine is still winding up.

Mission: Intercept Unknown Inbound Suspect Aircraft
Heading three-one-zero, eighty miles south of Bimini, 1845 local
Two minutes have elapsed since the warning. Two minutes with weapons loaded, doors latched and locked, radios set, equipment and crew strapped in, headsets on.

The Customs Cessna Citation rolls south on a makeshift taxiway (inactive runway) at Home-stead Air Force Base (AFB) and the pilots complete scramble systems checks. She rolls past imposing rows of Reserve F-16 fighters on the left and Huey helos performing "drop" training on the right. Two F-16s are on five-mile final.

Just short of the active and still rolling, Carl Craig the copilot, switches the radio to tower frequency.

"Homestead Tower, Customs Five Seven ready for immediate takeoff, runway zero five."

"Roger, Customs Five Seven you're cleared for takeoff, runway zero five. The winds are at zero-nine-zero, seven knots. Say direction of turnout."

"Right turnout, clear for takeoff, Customs Five Seven."

"Mako One and Mako Two, break out and re-enter, Customs scramble."

The Mako Lead F-16 immediately pitches right for a 360-degree turn to clear the takeoff and departure corridor. The multi-million-dollar Customs Citation slows briefly to make a left turn onto the runway, then adds full power and accelerates. Seconds later, it is airborne. The gear is raised and the jet snaps hard right towards the ocean and Bimini.

The scramble to "wheels in the well" took five minutes and thirty-five seconds.

"Let's go hunting!" says the pilot between his teeth. The mangroves and coastline streak under them in a diminishing blur of green and blue; a

Customs aircrews head out to the ramp on a midnight run to assist a law enforcement effort against air smuggling. Scott Thode, JB Pictures

coastline Customs has sworn to protect from the insidious invasion of illegal drugs.

The Intercept
Over the Caribbean, 1910 local

The Citation, under the expert control of Rich Bowen, a veteran pilot of twenty years, cruises southeast towards Orange Cay, a little atoll south of Bimini. The pilots keep constant communication with C3I, the Command, Control, Communications and Intelligence Center in Miami, who coordinate the interception. If the target suspect is confirmed as a doper, C3I will assist the law enforcement effort to make an arrest.

Wally Goff, the AIO (Airborne Intercept Officer) in the back sensor portion of the cabin, fires up the F-16 FCR (fire control radar) and FLIR (forward-looking infrared). The radar's capabilities include line-of-sight acquisition and automatic lock-on of designated airborne and ground targets up to eighty miles away.

The radar equipment, built into the nose of the Citation, gives the jet a kind of "Snoopy" look. The actual infrared camera is fitted under the fuselage, providing a 360-degree look-down view of the aircraft's position. Precision and hand-eye coordination are required to effectively coordinate the use of radar and FLIR in tracking drug targets. A bluish-grey, monochrome image

Plugged into the APUs (auxiliary power unit) the alert Citations stand ready to roll within three minutes of the initial launch warning. The Citation is capable of going after a drug smuggler at 350 knots and slowing down to 90 knots for the intercept via extension of speed brakes on each wing.

Two red phones behind the ops counter at the Miami Air Branch, link the CDO (command duty officer) to C3I and the base tower. If the C3I phone rings, it is a harbinger for rapid action. The other phone is used to advise the tower of an impending launch. Scott Thode, JB Pictures

appears on the FLIR scope, while on the look-down radar scope the scanner sweeps back and forth, searching for bogies and targets of opportunity. The AIO guides the exterior camera by rolling his palm over a half-submerged ball, while he controls the radar, using a "stick" with fingertip controls for radar elevation, azimuth and range. Two green repeater scopes depicting the same images are mounted in the cockpit for the pilots.

The blue-green waters of the Caribbean begin to darken as the clouds and sky turn pink and yellow with the approaching sunset—a glorious sight.

Suddenly the headsets crackle with a call from C3I.

"Customs Five Seven, target one three zero at fifty-five. Heading two six zero."

Carl Craig, the copilot, acknowledges the call. "Roger. One-three-zero at fifty-five. Say angels [altitude]."

The AIO's (Air Intercept Officer's) station in the rear portion of the Citation's cabin has a fire control radar screen on the left and a forward-looking infrared screen on the right. Identical repeater screens are mounted in the cockpit for the pilots.

The Citation's F-16 radar has the capability of locating a target whose radar cross section is no more than 1 by 1.5 meters square at forty miles! The heat-seeking FLIR sensors transform the target into thermal images depicted on the screen, which also displays the changing closure rate between the two aircraft, airspeeds, altitudes, distance to target and intercept geometry prior to the intercept.

"Unknown."

Bowen immediately pitches up, realizing that his original heading puts him on a collision course. "Five Seven's coming right to one-one-zero and climbing to seventy-five." The turn will allow him to lead the target (ahead of his direction of flight) and the jet climbs to get above the target, whose altitude is as yet unknown. Leveling out at 7,500 feet, he leaves the throttles at max power to pick up airspeed.

"Customs Five Seven, you've got traffic at one-four-zero at ten miles. A Continental 727 descending to ten thousand feet."

"Roger," says Craig. "Fifty-seven's looking. Ok, I've got him, one o'clock high."

"Yeah, I see him. No problem," affirms Bowen, stabilizing the aircraft at 250 knots indicated.

The sky melts into vibrant gold as the Citation closes the distance to the target. The tension and excitement begin to mount.

An unbidden comment from one of the pilots comes to mind. "These guys [dopers] are almost brilliant in their endeavors . . . but completely lacking in conscience."

"Rich, I'm starting to pick up something on the radar," calls Wally Goff.

"OK." He keys the mike to C3I, "Bogey Dope [target info] for Fifty-seven."

"Roger Five Seven, target one-two-zero at twenty. Showing two thousand five hundred, unconfirmed."

After target information is relayed to the Citation, the decision to track that aircraft is left to the judgment of the Customs aircrews. In this case they followed him to Bimini where the guy landed and was busted. Intelligence, confidence, proficiency, professionalism and incredible flying skills are required for a safe, undetected intercept of an airborne drug smuggler.

"Copy, one-two-zero at twenty."

A few seconds later, "I've got him now!" exclaims Goff. "Twenty mile scope, one-two-zero at nineteen, two point five."

"OK, lock him up. Carl, I'm coming out of seven-five for three-five."

"C3, Five Seven's out of seven-five for three-five."

"Roger, Five Seven."

"All right Carl, you've got those great fighter-pilot eyes, do you see him yet?"

"Nothing but damn clouds, the haze is really bad."

"One-two-zero at fifteen—locked," reports Goff.

The aircrew are all looking, intent on a visual sighting of the target. They know that if he is a doper he'll be flying without lights, and against the blue-black water he'll be next to impossible to find from a look-down view. Bowen scans his instruments, assesses that Wally has a positive lock-on and calls C3I.

"C3, Customs Five Seven will take Judy on the target," meaning that he has a positive radar acquisition and will take responsibility for the intercept.

"Roger, Five Seven, Judy."

According to the scope in front of him, the target is ten degrees left of the nose, slightly low, about twelve miles out, with closure speed between the two aircraft at 350 knots. Their communication monotones do not compute with the scenario. They are flying on the ragged edge of what could become, within seconds, a deadly chase, yet they seem unaffected.

"Rich, I've got him on the FLIR," says Goff.

"I'm coming left," states the pilot calmly.

The Chase
Southwest of Bimini, 1945 local

"Tally Ho," calls the AIO. "Eleven o'clock low, just passing that cloud."

"Got 'im," Bowen affirms in a voice that turns to flint as he eases out of the turn six miles behind the target.

"C3, Five Seven's got a Tally Ho." The center acknowledges the visual. Meanwhile, a Customs Black Hawk, forty miles away on routine patrol looking for "go-fasts" (boats) and low-flying aircraft, is alerted and its pilot turns northeast to back up the Citation. Aboard the helo are five people who make up the bust crew: two male AIO's, a female AIO, a female DEA (Drug Enforcement Agency) agent and a Bahamian Defense officer.

"Four miles and closing at 180 knots," advises the AIO.

"Roger that," mutters the pilot between his teeth. The suspect aircraft is nothing but a speck of grey against the darkened waters. Bowen eases back the power, tightens up a left turn and gently lowers the nose as he rolls out behind the target. He quickly scans between the radar, the airspeed indicator, the altimeter and the airplane visually ahead.

"Two miles, closing at 150 knots," advises the AIO.

The sun has sunk in the horizon, leaving a wake of incredible oranges and reds smeared across the sky as Customs closes the gap at 2,300 feet above the ocean.

"One mile at 110 knots," says Goff.

"Looks like a low-wing twin—maybe an Aztec or Seneca," Bowen comments, easing back the power to idle.

A high-pitched sound blares in the cockpit at the same time that a red warning light flashes

Most often, a Black Hawk will join pursuit of an airborne drug hunter as seen from the window of a Citation II.

on the instrument panel. Carl reaches over to silence the gear warning.

The gap narrows between the nose and the bogey's tail.

"We're closing fast!" says Bowen as he fans the speed brakes out and back, bleeding off twenty knots of speed instantly. The Citation shudders just above a stall as the bogey begins to loom in the windscreen, fifty feet ahead and closing.

Bowen matches the airspeed, about twenty feet behind the bogey. Juggling and angling and cutting off to make a smooth transition, he tucks the nose slightly below and ten feet astern of the unsuspecting plane! The entire windscreen fills up with a menacing white Piper Aztec with dark-blue striping.

The veteran pilot holds his position, expertly handling the controls to remain in close, undetected formation behind the unwary plane. The situation is critical. There is no room for mistakes. His eyes are riveted to the horizontal stabilizer of the aircraft ahead.

Citations were designed for speed, comfort and pleasure. Forced into the Aztec's slipstream at landing speeds, the Citation does not fly

13

easily. Bowen can feel the buffeting of the twin's prop-wash on the rudder pedals under his feet. It's what they call close-trail formation. It's the same maneuver that the Blue Angels and the Thunderbirds use during their air shows, except that they know when the airplane in front of them will climb, descend, change speed or turn.

Bowen quickly scans the instruments—all in the green—and back again. "I'll put the numbers on your side, Carl," he says.

Bowen swings the Citation gently, about five to eight feet, to the right of the twin's tail so Carl can see the three-inch numbers high on the rudder fin: "November, five . . . two-zero . . . three . . . sh—! I missed the letter."

Bowen swings the Citation back to the right and says, "OK, take another look."

Carl Craig cranes his neck to catch the last letter as Bowen swings out again, eight feet below the Aztec.

"Yankee! November-five-two-zero-three-Yankee. I'll call it in."

While in undetected close trail to a smuggler aircraft, the intercept pilot will swing out about ten feet to read and identify the numbers on the target airplane.

While the copilot calls in the numbers to C3I, Bowen moves the throttles back an inch, presses the yoke slightly forward and slides back out, about fifty feet in trail into a looser, easier formation. A thin layer of sweat covers his forehead and temples. It leads one to wonder what a close interception would be like "in the weather."

The aircrew silently waits for confirmation from C3I on what they all sense, by sheer gut-feel, is going to be a harrowing chase.

With no warning, the Aztec noses down and banks right.

Bowen follows him, maintaining equidistance and speed. At this point it is absolutely crucial that the suspect pilot does not see the Customs aircraft. If he does, and if he is a doper, he will unload the drugs into the bottom of the ocean, ridding himself of incriminating evidence.

"He's heading north, three-zero-zero," notes Bowen quietly. "Looks like a Bimini run." He follows, flying just above the suspect aircraft as the Aztec descends through 1,500 feet.

Suddenly C3I breaks into the headsets.

"Customs Five Seven, suspect aircraft November-five-two-zero-three-Yankee confirmed stolen! Repeat. Suspect aircraft confirmed stolen."

"Roger, confirmed stolen. He's heading towards Bimini, three-zero-zero twelve hundred feet, descending. We're in trail."

"Copy. We've alerted the Black Hawk, heading one-five-five, twenty-five miles."

The last remnants of daylight give way to a violet, hazy dusk. There are no lights visible on the Aztec, forty feet ahead. The cockpit of the Citation is enveloped in a gentle red glow of the cabin lights. At 800 feet the twin levels out for what the Customs aircrew suspects is a drug drop.

"Wally, you looking for boats?" asks Bowen.

"Yeah, looks like we might have something . . . uhh . . . can't pick up the paint yet, but I'm getting a possible indication. Wait! Got it! Two, no, three surface targets, three-zero-five at eight miles."

"OK, let's see if that's where he's headed."

As if in answer to Bowen's comment, the

Aztec banks and descends. The Citation stays on its tail.

"C3, target aircraft descending through 500 feet. We've got three, repeat three, surface targets, five miles. Looks like a drop setup."

"Roger, Five Seven. Helo is one-six-zero, twenty miles, Angels one point five."

The Drop
Southwest of Bimini, 2005 local

"Rich, he's lowering his flaps," the copilot warns.

Bowen coaxes the power back on the jet—a jet that was never intended to cruise on the shuddering, buffeting edge of a stall at ninety knots, 300 feet above the ocean.

"Customs Fifty-seven, Cobra Two. We've got you. Contact on the nose, seventeen miles, three hundred feet," the Black Hawk advises.

"Roger Cobra Two. Looks like this guy is gonna drop. We've got three boats. Victor shaped lights, two miles."

One of the classic setups for an open-water drug drop is for the dopers to designate a position for the speedboats to idle, lights on, in an open V pattern. The doper aircraft then flies to that position and orbits, making as many passes as needed to drop the contraband in the center of the V.

"Rich, first orbit coming up, he's banking left, doors are open!" warns the AIO. Bowen pulls the nose up and climbs to 1,000 feet.

It is almost dark as they watch the Aztec roll left and down for the first drop. Visibility is nil with the exception of a vague line designating the horizon. Hopefully, the noise of the twin's engines, coupled with the inboard motors of the ocean cruisers, will drown out the Citation's noise, and the boat crews will remain unaware of Customs' presence overhead.

Bowen maintains altitude at 1,000 feet, but follows the twin's orbit 800 feet below. His maneuver will allow Wally to keep the FLIR camera on the drop, taping the sequence and enabling him to count the splashes. Later, the tape will be reviewed for evidence on the VCR at Homestead.

"He's dropping!" says the copilot, intent on watching the scope. "Two, three, four . . . six . . . eight. Eight bundles with glow sticks."

"Ok, let's see if he makes more," says Rich as he keys the mike to C3I. "Center, Customs Five Seven. We have positive drops. Stand by for coordinates."

Craig hands him the numbers, which he's read off the inertial navigation system, and Rich calls them in. "Position: north, two-five-four-niner-point-five. West, seven-niner-four-six-point-seven. Over."

"Roger . . ." they acknowledge the coordinates. "Cobra Two is one-six-zero for ten miles."

The Aztec makes a second and third pass. Craig counts eighteen bundles dropped in total. They look like bales of marijuana, but it's hard to tell for sure. C3I has alerted the Coast Guard and the Florida marine patrols. If the boats head for Miami or the Keys, they will alert state patrols, local police and the sheriff's office.

"Rich, he's turning north, three-zero, climbing," says Goff.

Military uniforms, gear and weapons are standard issue for all Hawk aircrews. These warriors don their gear and weapons and walk out to the aircraft with the same ease with which a businessman grabs his briefcase and walks to a commuter bus. Scott Thode, JB Pictures

Visibility from the armor-plated cockpit seats of a Hawk is almost unlimited. The chopper is fast enough and agile enough to stay in trail with a smuggler aircraft. But, if the pilot gets too close, the doper will hear the rotor blades and be alerted to Customs' presence, which will prompt him to dump the drugs overboard.
Scott Thode, JB Pictures

"Roger, I got 'im, coming right three-zero."

"Customs Fifty-seven, Cobra Two, at your six o'clock, one mile, fifteen hundred feet. Say intentions."

"We're going to stick with him."

"Roger, understand Cobra Two will join you?"

"That's affirmative."

"Roger that," adds the Cobra Two commander. "We'll ride this mother in."

"Roger."

"Looks like the guy's heading for Bimini," Bowen transmits.

"Roger."

Once the doper pilot has made his drops, he most likely will head for one of the island airstrips. With the Black Hawk only minutes away, Bowen remains in trail and assesses his fuel status—two hours of fuel. He has enough fuel for two options and determines that the best course of action is to stay with the Aztec if he can, saying, "We're gonna nail this bastard," rather than the boats.

The Aztec levels out at 1,000 feet above the ocean—airspeed 150 knots. Rich levels out, one mile in trail, at 2,000 feet. The Black Hawk joins up and flys formation, 500 feet below the Citation.

It's pitch-dark now. A hot, moonless, scuzzy night with clouds drifting 1,500 feet above the water. Three unlit aircraft, within one mile of each other, are flying low level, stacked, in the dark. One of them is unaware of the other two. All three are headed for a small Caribbean island called Bimini. All three have armed occupants.

Just Another Night in Paradise
The C3I "War Room," 2035 local

While C3I alerts DEA and the Bahamian Defense Forces, the Citation and the Black Hawk follow the unsuspecting Aztec into Bimini.

Meanwhile, the three illegal speedboats head for south Florida shores, and Customs scrambles two Cessna 404s for added surveillance. Additionally, the Coast Guard is alerted and deploys their vessels to intercept the inbound boats.

Fifteen minutes later, the Aztec makes a brief call for Bimini traffic on Unicom and sets up for a straight-in approach. He lands in the dark and rolls to a forced stop as the sudden floodlights and gunsights of the Black Hawk, a DEA helicopter, and three Bahamian police vehicles converge on his position.

The Citation circles, as a communication link, advising C3I of the action on the ground.

The six members of the Black Hawk SWAT (Special Weapons and Tactics) team jump out and surround the Aztec. There is no gunplay (the penalties for trafficking in drugs are less than for shooting at law enforcement officers). The twin-engined airplane and the remaining dope (believed to be the pilot's personal stash) are seized and two individuals are arrested. DEA and the Bahamian officers secure the bust and take disposition of the smugglers. They remain on the island with the DEA helicopter. The remaining bust team members jump back in the Black Hawk, its commander confirms "Code Four" (the bad guys and aircraft are secure) and the helo lifts off.

Assessing that the situation is well under control and that Cobra Two is airborne again, Bowen keys the mike to the chopper pilot.

"They've got it, Ralph. We're outta here!"

"Roger," acknowledges the Black Hawk commander. "Let's go nail the boats."

Both Customs pilots, of their own volition ("This is fun. We get *paid* to do this.") decide to join the boat chase.

According to all the information that is now flooding into C3I, two of the boats have headed for the upper keys. The third vessel speeds inside the reef line in Biscayne Bay. Ten minutes later, it gets nailed by the Coast Guard at Kings Bay, a private cut surrounded by a country club resort. However, one of the smugglers makes a break and gets away, with Metro-Dade police hot on his trail.

The other two speedboats split up as they near the coast. One heads for Dynamite Docks, south of Homestead, and the other makes his way further south, to Key Largo.

The Black Hawk and the Citation split up, each following one of the boats. The 404s are recalled and Rich follows the southbound vessel.

Within minutes, a Customs maritime boat nabs the first craft with the help of the Black Hawk's powerful "night sun" as they pull up to the jetty at Dynamite Docks. Florida State Troopers have already seized the vehicle and arrested the driver who was standing by for the transfer.

Meanwhile, Rich Bowen, in the Citation, finds the second boat entering Angel Fish Creek in Key Largo and Wally Goff keeps him on the FLIR.

The Black Hawk is airborne for the third time in as many hours and heads south, following US 1. The Citation acts as the eyes and ears for all involved and maintains communication with C3I. For ten minutes the speedboat seems to be lost or playing games, going in and out of

Tracking a doper aircraft to his destination often involves coordination between several Customs aircraft. Both the Black Hawk and a King Air (seen in the distance) will take credit for this bust. Scott Thode, JB Pictures

The Miami Air Branch patch.

cuts through the mangroves, leading a merry chase for the two Customs boats now following in the dark. From the air it looks like a grey ballet. The maneuvers allow time for the Black Hawk to join pursuit.

Suddenly, the speedboat turns hard, into Jew Fish Creek which leads under the main highway (US 1) to Key West. He comes out on the Gulf side of Key Largo and swerves hard left. A waiting van, onshore, signals him with his headlights and the smuggler runs the boat up on the beach. Within a heartbeat, all hell breaks loose!

The Black Hawk pins the scene with its powerful floodlight, the Customs boats train their lights on the beach and seconds later the Monroe County Police, blue lights flashing, dust swirling, come screaming down the only access road to the beach.

It is over. Time: 2142 local.

Wrapping It Up

With a bit of imagination, the Customs statement could have read like a scene out of *Miami Vice*, but it was written by Rich, a professional Customs officer, not a script writer.

The statement began: "On XX July, 1990, I was the pilot-in-command of a Customs Citation . . . ." and went on to give the intercept and arrest particulars: time, position, speed, heading, altitude, agencies involved, and so on. All very cut and dried. Very matter-of-fact.

It bore little resemblance to the hair-raising, mind-bending and sweat-drenched flight they had been strapped into two days before. It was hard to believe that three hours of precision aerial maneuvers had been reduced to two pages of boring, routine, black and white statistics.

The bottom line read: one aircraft seized—value $120,000.00; two vehicles seized—value $13,000.00; three vessels seized—value $210,000.00; ten individuals arrested; 1,400 pounds of marijuana seized; and 216 kilos of cocaine seized.

When the bales were broken open and weighed, Customs agents found six two-kilo bricks of cocaine in each bale. The totals represented $700,000.00 of marijuana, and $5,400,000.00 of cocaine.

Not bad for one night's work.

The trouble is, you see, statistics indicate that five to six times these amounts came into south Florida that same night.

It's a never-ending story.

Chapter 2

Miami Customs Air Branch

A Few Facts

Cocaine sells for up to $25,000 a kilo, wholesale, on the streets of the United States. That's big money. Unfortunately, the relatively small investment and risk involved in transporting it by air does not begin to compare with profits gained. For the job, the dopers prefer light twin-engined airplanes such as Piper Aztecs and Senecas, and Aero Commanders. The planes are readily available for sale or for the taking (as is too often the case) at any airport. They are almost always gutted and reconfigured with makeshift, long-range fuel tanks. Waterbeds, full of fuel and rigged with cheap plastic tubing, have been known to line the entire floor of a plane's passenger compartment as auxiliary tanks for a long haul.

Most of the flights originate in Colombia and can easily transport 500 kilos (1,200 pounds) or $12,500,000 worth of cocaine, on one trip. Depending on the drugs and the destination, the shipments are sometimes broken down into several flights. Marijuana is usually delivered in bales and coke in bricks packed in duffel bags.

The contraband is then dropped at low altitudes from smuggler planes at prearranged spots on land or water. These methods are only a few of those most commonly used by dopers on the shorelines of America and its Caribbean neighbors. Suffice it to say that their ingenuity

is a testimony to obscene greed and a complete absence of morality.

A record 17,685 pounds (7.89 tons) of cocaine were seized by US Customs in south Florida and the Caribbean in fiscal year 1990. It's a drop in the bucket compared to totals ending up on the streets of American cities across the nation.

The Outfit

Headquarters, US Customs Miami Air Branch, is located on a rather remote and anonymous northwest corner of Homestead AFB, Florida.

A more innocuous scene would be difficult to contrive. Customs operates out of a mishmash of nondescript buildings, pastel trailers and hangars, some of which are obviously vintage, military leftovers.

The general impression is one of incongruity. Rows of brightly colored general aviation and corporate airplanes line the flightline. With the exception of the Black Hawk helicopters, most of these aircraft have no resemblance whatsoever to the imposing, high tech, military aircraft one is used to associating with Air Force bases. Furthermore, there is no apparent rank and protocol. The women, and especially men, of the Air Branch are as laid-back and casual as any group of people at any fixed-base operation, in any civilian airport. Or, so it seems.

This gossamer veil actually shields a group of professional airborne drug hunters, for lack of any other apt description, most of whom are experienced, ex-military aviators. Many are combat hardened, having been pumped through the Vietnam pipeline. With 3,000 to 6,000 flying hours under their belts, they are as dedicated and serious about their jobs as any committed team of specialists and professionals anywhere.

Customs pilots are a special breed. They have a reputation for being nonconformist, hardnosed rogues with flying skills to match their aggressive, daredevil attitudes. There is not much that daunts these guys. There is nothing that gives them more satisfaction than seeking out, intercepting, tracking, pursuing, and successfully nailing dopers attempting to smuggle drugs into our country.

It is a job for which qualification does not come easy. At GS (Civil Service) ratings of 11 and above ($35,000 to $60,000 per year), the full-time pilots hold fixed-wing (prop and jet) ratings, with most being dual-qualified in helicopters. As criminal investigators, they are fully qualified within the US law enforcement system and maintain up-to-date training in a wide variety of

Customs' primary alert interceptors are the Cessna Citation IIs (C-550). They have a wingspan of fifty-two feet and are powered by two Pratt & Whitney jet engines which give the airplane 4.5 hours of endurance at 262 knots. The Miami Air Branch employs four Cessna Citations, two of which are always on alert and ready to launch against air smugglers attempting to deliver drugs to the United States.

firearms, special assault techniques and self-defense.

The man who oversees this rugged group of individualists in Miami is appropriately known as "Mad Dog." Roger Garland, chief of the Miami Air Branch, likes his job and his crew. (Garland has since been promoted to director of C3I at Air Ops East.) He should, he helped to hand-pick them. "After a six-month selection process of hard competition for available slots," Garland explains, "the pilots come onboard for about seven months of on-the-job training which allows them to become combat ready, so to speak, for the mission.

"The few older (fifty to fifty-five years of age) pilots got grandfathered in when there were no age restrictions, but now the limit is thirty-five years, which insures us at least twenty years of service from a new hire before retirement."

Since 1983, all the new-hires have been ex-military, and approximately forty percent of

"You cannot quantify deterrence at the air interdiction level," says Supervisor Larry Karson, who is shown briefing his crew for a mission. "If they take away the Air Branch tomorrow, the dopers will be back in full force the next day!" Scott Thode, JB Pictures

Air Intercept Officers and Bahamian Defense officers make up the Black Hawk bust teams at Miami. Their primary weapons are AUGs, rifles and shotguns.

those are still Army, Navy, Marine or Air Force Reservists. It wraps around for everybody; the US Government buys back millions of dollars spent in training and experience, and the aircrews get to keep doing what they do best—fly and fight. Flying for Customs is as close to combat flying as these pilots will get outside of war. They fly against real bogies in real intercept profiles, and although they don't actually shoot them out of the sky (yet), the risks are high as they remain in close control until the dopers are forced down and arrested.

The Miami Air Branch is the largest in the country and operates twenty-four hours a day, seven days a week with a detachment in Puerto Rico. They employ eighteen aircraft, fifty pilots and thirty-one AIOs who run the airborne radar sensor systems and carry the brunt of surveillance and tracking responsibilities.

The aircrews rotate on alert duty and, depending on the mission, they will fly one, two or even more aircraft if needed.

By sheer visual presence, the most imposing of these are the Sikorsky Black Hawk helicopters. Accommodating up to eight people, with forward speeds of 190 knots and vertical capabilities of 3,000 feet per minute, they are extremely successful in aerial pursuit and ground busting of the dopers. The shiny-black choppers, appropriately nicknamed Coke Busters, are the pride and joy of the unit. Stenciled on the fuselage are green (for "grass") and white (for cocaine) marijuana leaves attesting to the number of drug busts, the worthiness of the aircraft and the merits of the aircrews who fly it.

Other mission aircraft available to the alert crews include four Cessna Citations, one Beechcraft King Air, five Australian Nomad 88s for maritime surveillance, five Cessna 404s and one Cessna 206.

The Black Hawk is the pride and joy of Customs air. Imposing and intimidating, some Hawks are finished in high-visibility black and gold varnish schemes. With forward speeds of 190 knots and vertical capabilities of 3,000 feet per minute, they can easily accommodate a crew of eight—two pilots and a bust team of six.

The Nomads are optimized for the maritime patrol with a 360-degree radar system plus an infrared detection system. The Citations have been reconfigured with high tech, fighter interceptor radar systems and an extremely accurate INS (inertial navigation system), plus state-of-the-art radar and FLIR tracking systems and scopes. The systems are identical to those used by the F-16 fighters sitting on the Reserve and Air Force ramps on the other side of the base.

Garland candidly points out that "we have over $60 million of assets sitting on the ramp, plus another fifteen to twenty inside the building. In fact," he points to the Seizure Status Board in the ops room, "this board shows where all our money is. This is the reason that taxpayers are spending X-million dollars. The bottom line is right here; dope on the table, arrests, aircraft, vehicle and cash seizures. This is the end result of all the taxpayers' money spent on illegal drug interdiction."

The board reflects the past ten months, from December 1989 to October 1990. The unit had bagged five aircraft, four vehicles, fourteen vessels, 4,366 pounds of marijuana, a record 17,685 pounds of cocaine and $1,135,103.00 in cash, with 151 arrests. As big as the numbers were, they represent the little Dutch boy with his finger in the dike against the onslaught of illegal drugs entering the United States. All were successful drug interdictions, yet they accounted for less than 10 percent of the estimated totals transported into the country during those same ten months.

To more effectively fight the war against drugs, the unit needs more pilots, aircrews and aircraft.

Rich Bowen explains that despite some recent additions of aircraft to the fleet, "We are always politicking for more aircraft. Last month we put in 600 flying hours, and that's low for us.

The shiny black helicopters are appropriately nicknamed Coke Busters. The Hawk's "night sun" is a powerful floodlight used to light up night bust scenes to Customs' advantage.

When Customs missions involve a controlled delivery, the aircrews brief all the particulars available to ensure safety and success. When they sit alert and launch on an unknown suspect target, they dispense with briefs, rely on their knowledge, experience and training, and then debrief the mission. Scott Thode, JB Pictures

We would like to see 800 hours. With fixed-wing airplanes going in for inspections every month, it doesn't take long to wear the operational aircraft out. We're trying to get more aircraft. Unfortunately, political and monetary considerations often supersede threat priorities."

"Yeah," affirmed Garland, "this is no country club flying operation. We need more airplanes to operate effectively. To make more dope seizures."

The Customs mission is to detect, sort, intercept, track and apprehend the smugglers. "In 1990," said Garland, "even with our limited number of aircraft on line, we intercepted most of the suspect targets picked up by Customs radar units at C3I in Miami. But, C3I does not see all targets, there are too many soft spots."

Customs carries the greatest burden of fighting cocaine, mainly because it comes in by air and it comes in fast. Detection, however, is only the first hurdle of interdiction accomplished by Customs personnel at the Customs war room inside the confines of C3I. Positive radar and visual contacts are constantly being made across the country through NORAD, DoD (Department of Defense), and law enforcement intelligence channels, plus the FAA (Federal Aviation Agency), Civil Air Patrol (CAP) and

The west wall of the ops room at the Miami Air Branch is covered by a map of South America, the Caribbean basin and the southeastern United States. Behind the counter the duty officers monitor and attend to all communications. A Seizure and Case Status Board lines the north wall and an Aircraft and Aircrew Status Board is displayed on the east wall (not shown). The door in the back leads to a small computer room where access to classified information such as TECS (Treasury Enforcement Communication System), PAIRS (Private Aircraft Inspection Reporting System) and SATIN (Strategic and Tactical Intercept Network) is available at the punch of a button.

Customs Australian Nomad 88s, optimized with radar and infrared detection systems, are employed in maritime patrol and reconnaissance missions throughout US coastal areas.

Miami Black Hawk Drug-Warrior patch.

DEA personnel can be part of the alert crew for the Customs Black Hawks as they, not Customs, "run" the Bahamas. However, a Bahamian Defense officer, per international law, must be present at all times for Customs to make an arrest in the Bahamas.

Despite the casual appearance of the group, a trained eye would not miss the slight bulges concealing the firearms carried by all, the arsenals of portable firepower in odd corners of the room or the flight bags strategically placed by the door.

There is sound reasoning behind the seemingly civilian appearance. "Many times," says Rich Bowen, "we end up going into civilian airports—either following an airplane in, having to divert, or stop for fuel. We like to maintain a low profile, disguising who we really are. We don't like to advertise. It protects us and the people around us. The FBO people know that we *belong* to somebody, but they don't really know for sure until we're ready to leave and sign for the bill. The regs state that only the Black Hawk aircrews have to wear flight suits, camouflaged BDUs and rank."

The crews spend hours upon endless hours on alert, waiting for something to go down. It had been on one of those days—a lazy, stifling, hot afternoon—when the mission described in the first chapter was flown. The crews had been advised that "there might be some action." They had heard this before. In fact, the crews hear it all the time. Every day. Nevertheless, via nebulous electronic wizardry, criss-crossing the entire Caribbean area out of C3I, and some "prior intelligence," indications were that "there was something going on." The particulars had been briefed behind closed doors and the aircrews were ready.

Customs flying positions are not exactly cushy flying jobs. The pilots and aircrews never quite know what they are going up against. It is not easy keeping up with the creative and innovative methods that the smugglers use to transport their insidious cargo, and it doesn't get easier with experience. It just gets more frustrating. Customs pilots, aircrews and agents are warriors fighting a losing battle.

concerned civilians. With hundreds of suspect targets being sorted every month, Customs Air is charged with the task of scrambling to intercept, positively identify and appropriately respond to all suspect targets.

Pulling Alert

The alert aircrew at Homestead seems an unlikely sort for the job. Dressed in civvies, working at their desks or casually sitting around the ready room—the "Bat Cave"—leads one to wonder who they really are.

With the exception of some camouflaged trousers and a Bahamian Defense officer in full fatigues, they resemble, and are as laid-back as, a civilian group at a fixed-base operation (FBO). Legs outstretched, heads back, watching television or telling jokes, the DEA and Customs officers quip back and forth while brown-bagging, munching on Kentucky Fried, McDonald's or sushi. The only thing missing in this scene is the beer.

This seized Aero Commander used to belong to the Miami Air Branch. "Emily," as she was fondly referred to by the crews that flew her, was inexplicably painted bright blue and used for intercept training in the 1980s. The favorite old plane has since vanished off the flightline.

Chapter 3

US Customs Service: A Few Notes of History

The US Customs Service was formed under duress, on July 31, 1789, in an effort to save America's new and struggling government from financial collapse.

By an Act of Congress, authorizing President George Washington the appointment of Customs officers for the collection of import revenues for the central government, the thirteen colonies yielded their rights to collect and retain customs duties to the US Treasury. Within one year, the new Customs Service had collected over $2 million for the treasury which helped to establish financial stability for the fledgling nation and the credibility of the US Customs Service.

However, with the establishment of the US Customs Service came a historic problem associated with import and export laws and restrictions: smuggling.

The Origins of Smuggling

Smuggling is as old as recorded history, as old as recorded law.

As far back as Old Testament times, the scriptures document the use of tariffs and the inevitable evasion of taxes and customs duties by people of ancient times. In Europe, English history records the first customs collection of monies for vessels arriving at British ports in 979, and in 1217, the Magna Carta specified the "rightful collection of customs tolls" for merchants coming into and going out of the country.

Failure to comply with the law was met with strict penalties. Consequently, history tells us the professional smuggler was created. Since that time, his methodology and ingenuity have persisted. Evolving government vigilance and law enforcement efforts to quell smuggling have matched, but never surpassed the tenacity displayed or the success enjoyed by smugglers.

Smuggling, in North America, came with the advent of European merchants sailing into New World ports. In 1651, the first collection of customs was imposed by the Dutch at New York harbor on all foreign imports entering the city. In 1664, the city came under British rule and the continuance of the unpopular customs tariffs fueled smuggling endeavors for the next 100 years. In retaliation, England adopted tougher governmental policies on the Colonies which eventually led to the Boston Tea Party uprising in 1773 and the beginning of the American Revolution in 1775. Fourteen years later, after the Declaration of Independence and the subsequent establishment of the US Constitution, the US Customs Service came into being.

Smuggling in the United States

With the Embargo Act of 1808, brought on by the threat of American involvement in European wars, the United States began to contend with other domestic problems, a virtual halt in world trade, a depressed economy and a renewal of import goods smuggling.

Smugglers' ploys and devices, outside of high tech, have not altered much in the last 200 years. The coastal methods used in the 1800s were much like those employed today—running smaller craft back and forth from larger vessels, transfer of piecemeal cargo, concealing contraband in or under legitimate goods, false bulkheads, hollowed-out masts and spars, sinking and offshore floating of camouflaged contraband goods, documentation forgery, black marketeering and arrogant bribery.

Coastal smuggling, however, was not a singular problem. With US territories being extended across the plains and the Rockies to California, Customs officers were appointed to

The first US Customs air fleet consisted of Curtis Falcons flown out of San Antonio, Texas, in 1932. Tucson Air Branch

The Florida squeeze on drug trafficking in the 1980s forced the flow south to Puerto Rico. Customs, Coast Guard, Air National Guard and local law enforcement personnel search through thousands of ships for drug loads like this one. While Miami Coast Guard cocaine seizures were down by 8,000 pounds in 1990, Puerto Rico Coast Guard seizures increased by 20,000 pounds. USCG

collect territorial revenues due the US coffers. And, once again, effective avoidance of these laws resulted in a growing and prosperous illegal trade for smugglers.

By the 1880s, it was obvious that the Mexican border offered lucrative smuggling opportunities, and although Federal marshals were appointed to enforce local laws, it was not until 1854 that the first Customs post was set up along the border, in El Paso, Texas. Larry Karson, a Customs Supervisor at Miami who makes Customs history a practice said, "The Secretary of the Treasury had authorized the hiring of inspectors for horseback patrol duty along the border. These politically appointed, mounted inspectors became the first official Border Patrol of the United States. Although appointment authority rotated between Washington and the local Customs collector," Karson explained, "the collector was eventually allowed to hire veteran lawmen who included former Texas Rangers and ex-deputy sheriffs, and ex-calvarymen who had served with Teddy Roosevelt's Rough Riders."

From 1853 to 1933 all mounted inspectors reported to Customs collectors. In 1905 the appointment as a law enforcement officer was made available to all US citizens and in 1933, these officers were given the title of Customs port inspectors.

Also in the 1880s, cocaine was introduced to the United States and was hailed as a miracle drug, widely used in wines, toothpaste, soft drinks and a variety of medicinal "cures." It would be ten years before cocaine's addictive and destructive nature was revealed, and another fifteen years (1905) before it was removed from Coca-Cola and banned in the United States.

Other illegal and extremely popular items of interest smuggled across the Mexican border from 1850 to 1930 were contraband whiskey, firearms, counterfeit money, cattle, bandits and prostitutes. Lesser known items were opium, heroin, cocaine and marijuana. The contraband crossed river borders on bridges, rafts, boats, floats and men's backs; it crossed land borders on foot, horseback, mule trains, wagons, trains and motor vehicles. Eventually or inevitably, the contraband came across by air.

These types of scenes, early in the Florida war on drugs, became hallmarks of the Miami Air Branch. Miami Air Branch

A south Florida bust of a truck that was rented for a long-haul delivery yielded thousands of pounds of marijuana. Miami Air Branch

Airborne Contraband

The first known airborne smugglers were intrepid World War I veteran pilots who flew rickety biplanes ferrying illegal alcohol from Mexico to Texas. One of these maverick pilots was caught redhanded by mounted border inspectors on a remote strip south of Cotulla, Texas. That event marked several firsts for the US Customs Service: the first pilot captured by Customs, whose property became the first plane seized by Customs, which sparked the idea for the first plane used by Customs, which saw the emergence of the first two Customs pilots, who made the second arrest and seizure for the organization.

Thus were the shaky, somewhat unorthodox and unsanctioned beginnings of America's drug enforcement air force. As described by author Garland Roark, in his book *The Coin Of Contraband*, "The unrecognized air force chased and captured smugglers as far north as Amarillo, seized narcotics, and aided San Antonio officers in grabbing off many a planeload of liquor. Conner [Chuck Conner, commander of the Federal border patrol] and his flying horsemen of the brush had eight planes flying, and others on the

In 1979, Americans consumed 130,000 pounds of marijuana a day, much of which was brought in daily from Colombia on airplanes like this DC-3 loaded *with 10,000 pounds of dope and bound for Nevada.* Tucson Air Branch

ground which had been cannibalized for parts. Like the Texas Navy of the 1840's, the customs air patrol was entirely self-sustaining. A little piracy was resorted to perhaps, but that was incidental to a job well done."

Within twelve months, Conner's air brigade had confiscated thirty-five airplanes, and the effective use of airborne assets to combat border smuggling was indelibly engraved in Customs lore.

Yet, it was not until the 1960s that the US Customs would have an air force wholly dedicated to combating the drug smuggler's trade.

The Aerial Drug War

In the 1930s, marijuana was legal and its use, particularly in the Southwest, came under harsh criticism by the FBN (Federal Bureau of Narcotics), who manipulated a public opinion craze against the users, citing that they committed heinous crimes under the influence. During the 1940s and 1950s, possession of a marijuana joint became a narcotics crime and those found guilty were sentenced by the courts with two- to five-year prison terms. The defendants were

A watery grave in Bahamian shoals claimed this DC-3. It is one of hundreds of smuggler aircraft forced down by weather, pilot error and/or law enforcement aircraft. Aircraft such as this are all that is left to tell the story of unsuccessful narcotics trafficking attempts. This war is fought unlike any other war in US history. In the drug war, the adversary continues to maintain a strategic and luxurious advantage, unlimited funds and can afford to lose assets and personnel.

almost exclusively poor, uneducated folk who lived in shantytowns.

With complex political and social movements being the hallmark of the 1960s, an ever-widening trend for casual, "recreational" and social drug use swept across America. It created an insatiable consumer market for drugs. The demand was rapidly exploited by criminals who were more than willing to supply the market and capitalize on the returns.

By 1965, drug smugglers had turned to private aircraft as an effective means of border penetration and, by 1969, major unchallenged smuggling routes had been blatantly established along the entire southern border of the United States because Customs owned only one single-engined airplane.

To combat the incursion of illegal drugs into the United States, Congress (in 1969) approved funds for, and authorized a US Customs Air Interdiction Program to reduce the level of smuggling, increase the smuggler's risk and cost, and improve the detection and apprehension of smuggling by aircraft, boats and vehicles. By 1972, Customs had acquired eleven assorted fixed-wing aircraft, eight helicopters and twenty-eight pilots. The aerial drug war, however tenuous, had begun.

Initiated with a full-scale surveillance of airports, the aerial war on drugs targeted south Florida and in particular Miami International Airport. On the airport's northwest corner, better known as "corrosion corner," was the General Aviation Center. It had become a virtual smugglers' haven where nondescript aircraft from Latin America, flown by aerial narcotics traders or *contrabandistas*, were the norm. Miami's general aviation ramps and hangars were laden with vintage aircraft: converted B-25s and B-26s, DC-3s, Piper Cubs, Lockheed Lodestars and general aviation aircraft with foreign and domestic registrations, many of which were used to smuggle drugs.

The Use of Military Technology

In 1973 the Miami Customs Air Branch (then termed Miami Tactical Interdiction Unit) began operations in earnest.

The Customs Service fleet had grown to incorporate more military aircraft—four Navy S-2s with radar and infrared sensor systems and four Army OV-1Cs retrofitted with FLIRs, some of which were employed by the Miami air unit along with a few seized and refurbished single- and twin-engined aircraft.

It rapidly became apparent that successful narcotics interdiction required effective sorting, detection and tracking capabilities, and a communications network. The few successful apprehensions that were made were based on prior information, intelligence, seedy informants and a lot of luck.

In 1970, the Comprehensive Drug Abuse Prevention and Control Act was implemented which toughened the penalties for marijuana and other "soft" drug dealers but reduced the penalties for possession to a misdemeanor. The measure resulted in public leniency towards drug use and drug smuggling. Marijuana became the Vietnam of law enforcement, a battle the United States could neither win nor wholly abandon.

In July 1973, the DEA was formed and assumed investigative authority for illegal drugs, which allowed Customs to focus on patrol and interdiction efforts under a new Air Support Program. The program grew over the next five years to include units in New Orleans, Louisiana; Houston, San Antonio and El Paso, Texas; Tucson, Arizona; San Diego, California; and, later, other cities along the Atlantic and Pacific coasts. Additionally, two internal data systems—PAIRS (Private Aircraft Inspection Reporting System) and TECS (Treasury Enforcement Communications System)—and other assets were installed to assist Customs in identifying, sorting and interdicting smuggler aircraft. By 1976, Customs had its first Cessna Citation, a sensor-

A Cessna 206 and its doper aircrew met with more than they could handle when they attempted to evade a Tucson intercept aircraft. Tucson Air Branch

equipped, high-performance corporate jet assigned to the Tucson Air Support Branch.

Predictably, the smugglers' habits, routes and methods all changed with the advent of heightened Customs surveillance, detection and interception. They quickly changed their drug-running routes to more benign geographic environments, resuming illegal operations with renewed, if not blatant, vigor. Their cargo remained the same, cocaine and marijuana.

There were other constants that also became apparent during the initial stages of the high tech war on drugs. First, drugs were largely being smuggled in general aviation airplanes. Second, smuggler aircraft were being flown into the United States at very low altitudes. Third, military technology onboard the Citations had proved to be highly effective. Fourth, the importance of close cooperation with other agencies (DEA, CIA, FBI, FAA, DoD, Border Patrol and local law enforcement) was clearly identified as one of the success factors.

However, in fiscal year 1979, Customs operation arrests and seizures indicated that the *contrabandista*'s level of activity was on an alarming rise in the Caribbean basin and the south Florida region. Florida has 8,246 miles of shoreline, much of which is desolate, and hundreds of operational airports and abandoned or makeshift airstrips that are ideal for landing drugs. In spite of the Air Branch's high tech equipment and all-out efforts, it was estimated that they were interdicting only about 1 percent of the drugs.

Experts determined that 70 to 80 percent of drugs entering the United States were being channeled through the Florida peninsular corridor. The result was billions of narco dollars being laundered in Miami banks. Furthermore, these shipments were accompanied by prolific transfers of illegal automatic weapons. South Florida became a killing ground.

In 1982, the area was targeted by the Reagan administration for priority law enforcement, and the South Florida Task Force was formed with Vice President George Bush at the helm. A concentrated eight-year effort to reduce the drug flow by intensifying air, sea and land interdiction missions was conducted. The Coast Guard received Dassault-Breguet HU-25 Falcon jets for air interdiction and high-speed cutters for sea operations. Surface-effect ships (hov-

This smuggler aircraft was intercepted by a Citation. Suspecting a law enforcement trail, he attempted to rid himself of incriminating evidence and was instead photographed by an astute copilot while air-dropping loads of drugs over the water. Miami Air Branch

A US Customs Service patch.

ercraft) were moved to patrol choke points into Florida waters. New offshore vessels patrolled coastlines and Navy AEW (Airborne Early Warning) E-2C aircraft were tasked with full-time detection of smuggler aircraft.

The Miami Customs Air Branch hired more aircrews, received a fleet of Army "killer" Cobra helicopters armed with 30-million-candlepower spotlights for special operations and, in 1983, took delivery of Black Hawk helos to combat the growing surge of drugs.

The massive build-up of assets and agencies was not without its problems. When the Coast Guard joined the air war, overt attempts were made for Congress to eliminate the Customs Air Program on the coastline. What had previously been an excellent working relationship between Customs and Coast Guard, particularly in the field, was reduced to inter-agency rivalry. Turf wars erupted between them with public relation campaigns claiming their agency was better than the next guy's and that they were "on the front line of the drug war." Mudslinging became the norm. Jurisdictional duties were fought over. Vital information that should have been shared, was withheld for self-serving purposes. Operational tasking was coveted and jealously guarded. The media blew several classified operations by printing stories which alerted and worked in behalf of the bad guys. Other Federal agencies joined in the rivalry and claimed drug seizures made by Customs and Coast Guard agents. Controlled deliveries were bungled. Task Force efforts were nationally exaggerated, distorting the significance of seizures which aggravated drug warriors and analysts. The underlying factor for all the above was that in working towards a common goal, none of the agencies were reading off the same sheet of music! Basic communication, command and control were lacking.

If Customs or Coast Guard assets are not at the scene of a narcotics delivery during an actual Caribbean-area air drop or delivery, chances are they will never recover the dope or make any apprehensions. For this reason the aircraft are often prepositioned at NAS Guantanamo Bay, in Cuba. USCG

Even so, the South Florida Task Force seized hundreds of thousands of marijuana bales, thousands of pounds of cocaine, Quaaludes by the billions and millions of dollars' worth of aircraft, vessels and vehicles and made hundreds of arrests.

The little Dutch boy *had* made a difference! He had managed to plug the hole even if the dike sprung other alarming leaks.

By the end of the 1980s the drug smugglers had simply moved their illegal operations elsewhere—offshore, the Caribbean Islands, the Gulf Coast, the Southwest, the Midwest, the Eastern Seaboard and the West Coast.

Chapter 4

The Second Line of Defense

Effective air interdiction involves a chain reaction requiring five elements: detection, sorting, interception, tracking, and apprehension.

Detection is accomplished via extensive air- and ground-based radar surveillance followed by a complicated method of sorting legitimate traffic from illegitimate aircraft. Once this is accomplished, interception of the suspect target is effected, followed by tracking that aircraft to its destination. If all of the above has been carried out successfully, the drug runner and the contraband will be seized when they land.

Defense in Depth

With smuggling operations being spread out like soft butter on toast and channeled into cities throughout the nation, Customs devised a new interdiction strategy in 1988 called Defense in Depth. Adopted by the government, the concept provided offensive and defensive capabilities via the use of mobile and fixed detection resources, deployed in depth and reaching to drug source and transit countries from the borders of the United States. In lay terms, the attack on drugs at their source was to be the first line of defense. The attack on drugs in transit was the second.

Eight Customs aviation branches in strategic locations across the country and their eight aviation units, make up the second line of defense or front-line border defense. To gain a clearer understanding of their tactics, one needs to understand the basic strategy and goals of the first line of defense.

The first line of defense is military early warning aircraft that provide surveillance from international airspace of drug source countries in northern South America and Central America. Early detection offers intelligence for the second line of defense to organize and execute their mission. Also, if and when a suspect aircraft is identified at its point of departure in Central or South America, sorting that target from legitimate US traffic becomes an easier task.

Implementation of both the first and second line of defense in southeastern sectors of the United States and the Bahamas forced Colombian drug traffic to find alternative smuggling routes along the lower Caribbean and the Mexican-American border. Illegal activity in those areas clearly demonstrated that much of Florida's drug traffic had swung south to Puerto Rico and west to Arizona.

The Tucson Customs Aviation Branch

The mission of all Customs aviation operations is to disrupt and disable the air transportation system used to deliver drugs to the United States.

The Tucson Aviation Branch is one of four original aviation units established in 1971 for this purpose. Located at Davis-Monthan AFB, the branch operates out of new facilities with

The Tucson Air Branch at Davis-Monthan AFB uses a variety of general aviation aircraft for surveillance and reconnaissance purposes. Tucson Air Branch

The Tucson Air Branch patch.

eighty-three Customs personnel and fifty contract maintenance personnel who are commanded by Customs Branch Chief Jerry Young. (Jerry Young has since been promoted to director, Customs National Aviation Center.)

Tucson's area of operation has always been extensive, and back when the unit first began operations, "We started out with some seized airplanes," the chief explained. "Then, we went to the Air Force junkyard and got a bunch of target drones, Debonaires, Bird Dogs, S-2s, OV-1 Mohawks, O-2s and Hueys. By 1973 we were pretty well operational and, essentially, the first Customs fleet was a mixture of seized aircraft and junk that the military had thrown away. We flew those airplanes until maintenance on the aircraft became almost prohibitive. In 1976, we began looking for newer aircraft and that's how the Citations and the King Airs came into the inventory."

The first Cessna Citation was delivered to Tucson for testing in 1976. Today, four operational jets are employed by the branch and their unit detachment in Phoenix. The aircraft's top speed is rated at 350 knots, it has an endurance capacity of 4.5 hours and is their primary interceptor aircraft.

The branch also flies two Sikorsky UH-60 Black Hawks acquired in 1986, which have a five-hour endurance level and are night-vision equipped. They are used for surveillance, but their primary mission is for assault and apprehension of suspect drug planes, pilots and individuals.

"What we've done," said the chief, "and what we've tried to do, particularly with the Citation, is merge military assets with civilian aircraft. That is, go to a corporate aircraft that is cheaper, easier to maintain, a little bit more user friendly . . . and go to the military for the high dollar, high tech sensor systems, because nobody else is competing in that mission. That is, nobody else in the civilian aircraft business needs an F-16 radar."

When all the above was approved by Congress, "We were very small, we were very hungry and we were responsive," said the chief. "We took on our portion of the drug war with vigor and dedicated 100 percent of our time to the air war on drugs. It was our number one priority.

"We're out mingling with civilian smuggling aircraft and flying against their mission," explained Young. "To do that, we need the technology, the magic and the night-vision capabilities of the military. Instead of taking military aircraft to chase civilian airplanes, we took civilian airplanes with military technology to chase those planes. That merger is giving us cheap operational costs, ease of maintenance and high-tech information we require to get the job done. It has worked very well.

"Nobody else has a mission like ours," he continued. "The military's mission is to defend, to lock on and shoot down the enemy. Ours is to intercept, to lock on, track and arrest. For maximum effectiveness, we marry military technology with civilian platforms and save the taxpayer some money."

To augment the intercept mission of the high-tech aircraft, Customs air nationwide was integrated into NORAD's (North American Aerospace Defense Command) air defense and radar surveillance system in 1976. One year later they were incorporated into the FAA radar system and a year after that the first tethered Aerostat radars went on line. By 1988 the C3I

centers were fully operational. The last building block to the Customs air mission was to centralize their national aviation headquarters in Oklahoma, where CNAC (Customs National Aviation Center) is located, serving as the operational field headquarters for all Customs aviation operations.

Young explained that for acts of self-defense and arrest, all aircrews maintain standard US Treasury Department firearm qualifications, plus additional Customs qualifications involving special assault techniques. All of his pilots are required to be dual-qualified in fixed-wing and rotor aircraft. "Although it's a tough policy," states the branch chief, "it's not a hard requirement to meet. We adhere to that requirement at Tucson and try to take advantage of it to make sure that everybody flies both fixed-wing and rotors, and maintains proficiency in both areas, for several reasons. First of all, our missions are based on a team concept involving detectors, interceptors, trackers, and you can't perform the mission effectively without all the other players. Secondly, the more familiar the pilots are with the different individual aircraft's mission, the better the team works. Finally, a dual-rated pilot knows the assets available in all aircraft, he understands their mission, their capabilities and how to pass information back and forth. Thus, he is better equipped to handle the intercept mission in its totality."

All Customs aircrew members perform their day-to-day functions as a team under supervisors. The teams rotate periodically on three eight-hour shifts with two teams being on duty at all times, from eight to four, four to midnight and midnight to eight. Each shift has a different mission focus. The day shift carries the brunt for support requirements like case work, the evening shift is responding to sensors and the midnight shift is the usual graveyard shift, a lot of individual paperwork interrupted by sporadic alerts. All shifts undergo daily training to maintain their proficiency requirements for the Customs air mission and, via rotating the shifts every two weeks or so, the teams familiarize themselves with the cases and the full aviation program.

Tucson bust crews keep their gear close at hand for immediate launch against airborne drug smugglers.

The Smugglers' Offensive

The principal routes of air delivery used by drug smugglers reflect where the cargo is coming from and where it's destined. These routes are predicated, number one on US demand for drugs (primarily cocaine) and number two, on getting around the United States' high-tech, front-line border defense.

A typical flight will depart from a nondescript airfield in Colombia and fly north to the Caribbean, up the Atlantic Coast, over the Gulf, up the Pacific Coast or through Mexico into American airspace. They may or may not stop for fuel, but they will operate in such a manner as to avoid undue notice, evade radar detection and thus arrest. They are cunning, wiley, tenacious, resourceful and often exhibit risky but exceptional flying skills, particularly at night.

Once he approaches his destination, the smuggler pilot has a remarkable set of options available to deliver the goods; he can land on makeshift airstrips or operational runaways, he can air-drop over water or land, or he can make full use of the law in his favor. The last option is a favorite and effective technique along southwestern borders.

The method is basic. The smuggler makes an air drop to a vehicle in desolate Mexican desert areas and the drugs are then shipped overland to the United States. Or, he can air-drop just north of the border in US deserts, then hightail it back to Mexican airspace and be home free.

Home free? the reader may ask. Yes . . . *home free!* because present Mexican-American relations do not allow *any* US-registered aircraft to fly into Mexican airspace without a prior flight plan. Moreover, the Mexican government does not allow law enforcement or military aircraft to enter their airspace without prior notification and official permission, which involve lengthy bureaucratic processes. Any incursion is considered a violation of Mexican sovereignty and is subject to severe penalties, not to mention the negative political implications. And, because Mexico has neither the radar capability nor the resources to detect or intercept an airborne drug smuggler, the pilot is too often home free.

Dead in Their Tracks

Unfortunately, the efforts of the Tucson Air Branch, and its sister branches along the southwest border, are thwarted by this open link in the chain of interdiction which causes them to stop dead when tracking a southbound target. Exploiting that open link, a doper can be tipped off that he is being tracked in US airspace and make a 180 back to Mexico. Or, he may air-drop the goods and slip back into Mexico. Or, he may land

These photos from the Tucson scrapbook show drug busts in the 1970s and early 1980s when Americans consumed about 66,000 pounds of cocaine a year worth $20 billion. Scott Eshelman

in a remote strip, often made the night before, off-load the drugs, then fly back to Mexico. Or, he may suspect that he is being tailed and return to Mexico. Or, he can land fifty feet south of the border, or, or, or . . . .

Successful detection, sorting and launching of Customs assets to verify a suspect target, which is subsequently tracked back to the border, almost classifies that mission as non-effective. When all concerned watch that aircraft brazenly disappear into Mexican airspace, the mission becomes a glaring failure; a waste of money for US taxpayers and a maddening, humiliating and frustrating defeat for Customs warriors.

The Office of Aviation Operations states that its interdiction strategies are directed towards a goal which seems deceptively simple: to reduce the general aviation smuggling threat by 50 percent of its 1982 level by 1992. They further explain that the odds of success in the interdiction process can be measured on a graph and is explained as follows in *An Air Interdiction Primer:*

Armed go-fast crews are not that unusual in Puerto Rico. They can be bad guys, undercover agents or legitimate civilians protecting their life and property. Miami Air Branch

40

"From an entire population of, say, 1,000 aircraft, only 40%— or 400 aircraft—are detected. Of these 400, 90% are accurately sorted, leaving 360 aircraft from the original population (of suspect aircraft). If interception can be accomplished for 90% of these, then 324 aircraft could still be tracked and apprehended. Tracking might succeed 90% of the time, leaving 291 aircraft. Finally, apprehension is successfully achieved for 89% of those left after tracking, resulting in the seizure of 262 aircraft from an original population of 1,000 suspects. In this example the final success rate is approximately one complete apprehension in four attempts."

The presence of Customs defense resources and personnel nationwide has clearly been measured in far better numbers than those which were present in 1982. Their success is also proven by evolving smuggling routes when the threat of interdiction in a given geographic area becomes greater than the risks involved in transporting the dope through that area. However, in the southwestern scenario, because of Customs' inability to pursue a suspect into Mexican airspace, the final success rate reflects a number far less than one apprehension in four smuggling attempts.

One case in point, which the author witnessed in November 1990, while doing research with the Tucson Aviation Branch, was as follows:

Prior intelligence had indicated that an airborne smuggler was on his way to the United States with a load of drugs. His progress was carefully monitored throughout the day. When it became apparent that he was approaching American airspace, both the Citation and the Black Hawk were launched. Once the smuggler crossed the border, the Citation effected a successful intercept and a positive identification on the aircraft. Somehow, the smuggler was alerted (probably by CB radio) that he was being followed by Customs, and he headed back for Mexico as night fell on the desert. The Black Hawk joined the close pursuit and tracked the smuggler to a small Mexican border town named Naco. As both crews in the Citation and the Hawk orbited at altitude (in American airspace) and watched on the FLIR, the pilot landed his aircraft on a dirt runway, off-loaded the drugs, took off without lights and disappeared into the night.

It didn't make sense. Where were the Mexican *Federales* (federal police)? the author asked the branch chief. "Right now there is no way of making official, immediate one-on-one contact with Mexican law enforcement agents or agencies," he responded. "We have no authority to take law enforcement action in Mexico or its airspace, although the Customs commissioner is working on it. Also, there have been cases where US Customs aircrews have witnessed or monitored what is believed to be drug activity in Mexico. In those cases, they called the DEA, the DEA called Mexico, the Mexicans called out their *Federales* and the bad guys were busted."

In any case, failure to secure a working border airspace agreement between Mexico and the United States has resulted in Customs aircrews being forced to fight the war on drugs with one hand tied behind their back. It is the same bureaucratic mindset of the unfavorable terms in which American pilots fought the war in Vietnam, and we all know what the outcome of that conflict was.

Impact on the Legitimate Civilian Pilot

A couple of years ago, Arizona had the dubious reputation of being the number one state for aircraft theft. Stolen airplanes make up the bulk of the smugglers' fleet, and their methods of ripping off legitimate aircraft from legitimate owners were basic. A common sequence was to steal a single-engined, high performance airplane, such as a Cessna 210, from any given ramp, fly it to a remote strip in Mexico, load it up with marijuana, fly back to the United States, air-drop the dope, turn around and fly back to Mexico (as they flip the bird to Customs), land, and offer the plane to the Mexican drug ring in payment for the drugs.

Now, for all practical purposes, and according to US laws, the innocent US citizen—the owner of the airplane and insurance payer—was actually paying for a load of marijuana being delivered to the United States! Furthermore, until the plane was confirmed as having been stolen (which often took weeks), the smuggler pilot had free rein going back and forth across the border! To add insult to injury—it was all profit! Tax-free profit!

"The only people getting hurt," stated Young, "were the legitimate, innocent aircraft owners. Moreover, all the added FAR AIM [Federal Aviation Regulation laws governing civil aviation] changes that were implemented in the last few years . . . that hurt the legitimate flyer . . . were designed to help us sort the good guys from the bad guys who were blatantly abusing legitimate border rights on both sides!"

The smugglers' use of the Mexican border also led to a Mexican shoot-down policy. As the news of that action gathered momentum in the United States, it was met with much trepidation from legitimate civilian pilots. In fact, according to authorities with the FAA's Accident Prevention Program, some aircraft *were* actually shot at and disabled during takeoff and landing attempts in Mexico. The FAA was quick to add that investigations into these random incidents

The CHET (Customs High Endurance Tracker) is a Piper Cheyenne III retrofitted with an APG-66 radar and AAS-36 infrared detection system for day or night tracking operations. The aircraft, introduced to the Customs inventory in 1985, has an eight-hour endurance capability. Tucson Air Branch

had revealed planeloads of illegal drugs where pilots were attempting to evade Mexican authorities. The FAA notice did little to allay legitimate pilot concerns about filing Mexican flight plans or, worse yet, the consequences of innocently straying into Mexican airspace.

The chief cautioned against getting caught up in, or focusing on, a negative view of the war on drugs, and outlined some positive factors. The program has generated a public awareness program, revealed drugs to be killers, exposed

Air drops are a smuggler's preferred method of delivering narcotics to Puerto Rico. The Black Hawks and their bust crews run surveillance and patrol flights along the island's borders, looking for go-fasts. Scott Thode, JB Pictures

the violent crime generated by the drug market and changed the jurisdictional outlook. "If I took the criminal to court ten years ago," says Young, "I was the bad guy. Five years after that we were on an even keel. Now, when we take the smuggler to court, he is the criminal."

Puerto Rico Customs Aviation Unit

By mid-1990 it was obvious to law enforcement authorities that Puerto Rico had become the number one hot spot for air smuggling activity in the United States. That assessment began when the US Coast Guard found a ton-and-a-half of cocaine on a Panamanian freighter early in 1990. Five more tons were seized within months, and by October Customs alone had logged 1,866 known air drops and 198 (suspected drug related) aircraft crashes in or around the island of Puerto Rico!

Because the assault of illegal activity was more than anyone had anticipated, authorities were caught somewhat off guard and forced to quickly gear up all available resources and assets to combat air smuggling in the area.

Founded in 1984 with two Aero Commanders, the Puerto Rico Customs Aviation Unit at Borinquen is located on the northwest end of the island at Raphael Hernandez Colon Airport (formerly Ramey AFB for B-52s). The unit operates under the Miami Air Branch as a forward strategic base.

Customs supervisor Harry Betz heads up Puerto Rico's operation with eight full-time pilots and three full-time AIOs who are supported by rotational air and maintenance crews from the parent branch in Miami as well as other Eastern air branches. Dedicated aircraft available to the crews are two Nomads for maritime surveillance, two twin-engined Cessna 404s and one King Air. The Australian Nomads are four-place, twin-turboprop aircraft. They are normally operated by a pilot, copilot and an AIO who runs the radar and infrared sensors. Its top speed is 166 knots and it has four hours' endurance. The twins are employed in a variety of ways, from ho-hum utility missions to dangerous drug setups and busts. The aircraft are often backed up by Miami's Citations and Black Hawks.

"With the success of air-land interdiction efforts in south Florida," remarks Betz, "traffickers sought out less-threatening routes and turned to Puerto Rico. If you put pressure on anything fluid, that substance is going to squish out around the edges. We just happen to be one of those edges and Puerto Rico has become the hottest spot for cocaine smuggling encountered to date! The island is the main gateway for getting drugs from Colombia to the mainland, USA."

Authorities agree that with most of Puerto Rico's coastline unguarded, its proximity to Colombia (400 nautical miles from Guajira Penninsula) has made the island a smuggler's dream. Inadequate radar surveillance makes access in and out of the area easy—in fact, a piece of cake! The area has become the cartel's back yard where undetected cocaine air drops are "open season."

To complicate the issue, the island is a US commonwealth where, by law, Customs formalities for passengers and cargo traveling from Puerto Rico to the US mainland are not required. Once a load of foreign cargo has cleared Customs authorities in Puerto Rico, the shipment is considered domestic cargo.

Authorities further acknowledge that a lack of personnel restricts port search capabilities. About 70,000 ship entries are logged at the Port of San Juan each year. With an average of 4,000 cargo containers arriving at the port every month, only 15 percent of them are searched by Customs officials who rely on National Guard help to achieve even that small percentage.

That is the first nightmare. The second is air-dropping of drugs.

"It's like rain, tropical cocaine rain," claimed a concerned citizen. "Once the dope gets in here," adds Betz, "it might as well be in downtown New York or Kansas. If the narcotics make it to Puerto Rico, in most cases it's going to hit the mainland."

With over 2,000 air drops reported in the Caribbean area by Customs and DEA in 1990, it has become obvious that inadequate radar coverage is not only the number one problem for law enforcement agencies, it's their number one priority. But high-tech radars, on the ground or in the air, take money and time. With those considerations, full radar coverage is scheduled to be in place by late 1991. Until that time, doing anything to evade the law and dropping to speedboats will continue to be the drug smugglers' favorite ploy.

On one Customs mission, Nomad aircrews watched a smuggler air-drop to speedboats whose drivers panicked, hightailing it out of the area without picking up the load. As a Customs chopper recovered the bales of contraband, the Nomad chased one of the boats and watched (and taped) the smugglers run aground at high speed in an attempt to escape!

Two bad guys ended up in the hospital, confirming Harry Betz' claim that "these people will do anything in the world to get away from you. Jamaicans are the most violent," he added, "they will do anything. Colombians are potentially violent, the Cubans are pretty easy to deal with and Americans are a tossup." But no matter who they are, Customs always hopes that one of them will "roll over"—a bad guy turned informant. But, "you can't be worrying about what's going to happen to the guy after we get him," said the unit supervisor. "You do your job as best you can . . . and that's it. When it's not fun anymore, for whatever reasons, you don't do this job anymore."

The tough odds that Puerto Rico is up against require both short-term and long-term solutions to certain problems:

- Inadequate manpower and assets. Puerto Rico officials claim they need more assistance and a greater commitment from the US government to combat the drug problem—a problem exploited day-to-day by drug smugglers. Washington has promised more human and technological resources. However, that takes time. In the meantime, bright colored plastic bricks of cocaine are constantly being seized, attesting to the fact that the island is a major distribution steppingstone to US streets.

- Security. Customs has a "mini-C3I" at Port Salinas, but island radars and agencies will not be computer-linked until the end of 1991,

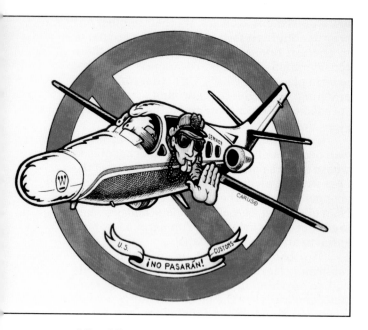

Miami-Puerto Rico Unit logo. Miami Air Branch

which causes communication and security problems. The unit is stationed on a public airport next to a public road which allows the bad guys some surveillance of operations and full surveillance of launches.

- Local forces are inadequate. Puerto Rican Forces United for Rapid Action (FURA), formed in 1986, began to assist the drug war under a Puerto Rican government drug interdiction program. That program is now run by the Puerto Rican State Police Department with FURA officers helping to make up for the lack of US personnel. They work side by side with other law enforcement agents on the island but the effort is new, not yet cohesive and not as effective as originally intended.

- Natural disasters. When Hurricane Hugo roared through the lower Caribbean, it also provided some advantageous situations for smugglers. The island was in complete disarray. Massive rescue efforts demanded law enforcement agencies to focus on humanitarian services, civil defense, disaster relief, and search and rescue responses. Three tons of cocaine were seized in the storm's aftermath, but officials estimate that six to seven tons got through, with deliveries stepping up shortly after.

- Beleaguered US personnel. Curtailing drug smuggling is a twenty-four-hour-a-day, 365-day-a-year job which has taxed, stressed, maxed out and worn out the too few special agents, port authorities, law enforcement officers and Customs personnel in Puerto Rico.

- No end in sight. "When we did our job in Miami in the 1980s," said Betz, "it resulted in pushing the flow of drugs off to the Bahamas. I predict that our efforts here will have that same effect to the south and the flow will eventually go down the Leeward Chain to the Antilles. And at this point, we're still two to five years from peak time because it's a new ball game down here. We can't stop. We have to keep fighting. Each one of us is contributing to provide solutions and deterrence for the problems here. But, those problems are US problems and we need help."

Chapter 5

Special Weapons and Tactics

US Customs' biggest asset is the quality of their personnel. The Customs aircrew member's biggest assets are his or her professional training, airplane, experience and weaponry.

Every Customs officer in Air Ops, pilot, copilot or AIO is required to carry at least one handgun at all times. Most of them carry two weapons and some carry three. The choice is up to them. The firearms vary from standard issue handguns to rifles, shotguns and semi-automatic submachine guns. Depending on the mission, the weapons are carried inconspicuously in hip, back, shoulder, boot or ankle holsters, or out in the open, slung menacingly on their shoulders.

When a Customs Black Hawk is launched, every member aboard is prepared for a worst-case scenario involving incoming gunfire. Training and preparedness for this type of situation is focused on Tactical Teams in the south. Customs' South Central Region consists of five states: Tennessee, Arkansas, Mississippi, Alabama and Louisiana. The New Orleans Aviation Branch serves as the main air interdiction entity for this region.

New Orleans Aviation Operations Branch (NOLA)

Based at Naval Air Station (NAS) New Orleans, NOLA personnel are crammed into a vintage, two-story military facility built to serve thirty people. Attached to a hangar, the building is home to eighty-nine Customs agents and administrative personnel whose area of responsibility encompasses thousands of miles of Gulf coastline ideally suited for air smuggling. Given that the Aerostats, unmanned, airborne surveillance balloons, are not yet operational in the Gulf states region, numerous waterways, bayous, inlets and canals, also free from law enforcement scrutiny, make ideal areas for aerial and maritime drug deliveries.

Despite the relative ease of coastal access, only about 100 aerial border intrusions were detected by Customs in 1990. Customs intelligence sources believe that those low numbers may indicate the lull before the storm. The Gulf threat, in terms of air smuggling, is a viable one and the marine threat remains enormous!

Normal helicopter activity alone—servicing offshore, foreign- and US-flagged vessels—is a potential all of its own. A typical Bell 206 Jet Ranger can carry a payload of 1,100 pounds over 300 miles without refueling. Under the cover of legitimate traffic, 6,000 helicopter sorties per day in the region, helicopter smuggling flights would be hard to detect let alone sort.

To combat both the existing and potential rise in smuggling activity, the New Orleans branch flies about 400 hours a month and employs a fleet of fifteen aircraft: two Citations, two Black Hawks, two Nomads, one Beech King Air, one STOL (Short Takeoff and Landing) aircraft, two Piper Navajos, one Cessna 210, two fixed-wing surveillance planes and two UH-1 choppers.

The branch is run by Bill Perry, a former supervisor from Miami. Prior to Bill's taking over as New Orleans branch chief in 1991, Louis Nunez was the acting branch chief. A Cuban by birth, Nunez fled in 1965 (on twenty-four-hour notice) with his family of seven by way of Spain to Miami. After his family relocated to New Orleans, Louis completed high school, joined the local police department, finished college and joined the US Customs Service.

NOLA operates under "a total team concept," says Louis, "a working relationship within

Some Black Hawks are optimized for covert night operations with light-deflecting, matte paint schemes.

shift groups, resulting in positive levels of bonding, knowledge of each other's performance and healthy competitiveness."

NOLA, like all the other aviation branches and units, works closely with other law enforcement agencies. Because the present day-to-day activity of air smuggling requiring air interdiction is low, AIO-criminal investigators at NOLA devote a lot of their time to case investigations. Coordinating intelligence and interdiction efforts in joint investigations with local law enforcement offices, many of these cases have been undercover operations requiring special weapons and assault techniques.

"Every officer in the branch goes through this type of training at least once a month," Nunez explains. "They are taught how to be aware of their surroundings on a takedown, how to make a correct approach, how to cover themselves, how to establish a perimeter and how to make the arrest as safely as possible. If we can take everybody down and make the arrests without getting anybody hurt and, without firing a shot—that's what we want."

Tactical Team

Mark Helton, an AIO and criminal investigator, is the overall tactical team trainer for the air branch. He joined the New Orleans Customs Aviation Branch as an AIO in 1988 after spending ten years as a law enforcement officer on patrol, on the SWAT team and in homicide.

"When I worked LE [law enforcement], 80 percent of our homicide cases were drug related," Helton said. "You can't work homicide without working narcotics." By the same token, Customs can't work counternarcotic air operations without law enforcement training and knowledge.

All Customs aircrews undergo tough training in the first year which is likened to a "baptism of fire." Much of that time is spent away from home—four months at a law enforcement academy and a short time with the Navy for water survival training. The AIOs attend a two-week course for sensor training in Corpus Christi, Texas, with the Singer Company (Allen Corporation Division), then they report to their home units where they undergo in-house, hands-on training. They used to spend a month at Marana airfield in Arizona for "special techniques," but "when Marana closed down in the late eighties, there was nothing to take its place," Mark explained.

Recognizing the need for some sort of program for effective takedown techniques, Customs officers at NOLA began doing some research. Information from Customs-wide debriefs yielded that plans, equipment and knowledge of the tactics used were standard. Because they had little prior or formal training on how to effectively conduct that kind of bust, the aircrews indicated a desire for more advanced and up-to-date techniques. Mark explained that, in accordance with existing Customs regulations, "we used to take four guys, jump out of a helicopter, and don't 'recon by fire' but catch all the bad guys, then handcuff the right ones!"

There was no book on how to do that effectively and safely, so Mark Helton and pilot Jim Esposito began devising a training program, generic to Customs' specific assets, mission and objectives. To do that, they borrowed SWAT and SOF (Special Operation Forces) unit techniques, mixed them with standard law enforcement and small unit patrol procedures and began training.

"Take a raid on a house, for instance," explained Helton, "using dynamic stacking. The stacking is nothing more than a military, small unit tactic where we line up, one behind the other, protected on one side by a wall-like surface. As we move forward, out into the open towards the objective, a 360-degree field of fire becomes available. We train low-ready position and do the same thing from the Hawk. It's an effective, safe and fast method to get from the Hawk to the bad guys, whose presence and position is preventing the bust aircraft from moving."

Tactical training at New Orleans is a relatively new program that has gained a lot of interest (and a certain amount of tongue-in-cheek infamy as NOLA Ninjas). "We're operating against sophisticated, defensive off-load plans backed by a lot of bucks, and whether they are gearing up for us [a Customs intercept] specifically, or the rip-off, is unknown. So, we train for,

and go into, an operation convinced that their tactics are designed to counter ours."

The "rip-off" refers to a common practice among traffickers where one group of bad guys, making a deal, selling or delivering drugs, will steal from their counterparts. These scenarios, involving millions of dollars, are just like those in the movies and are normally conducted by dopers without too much concern for human life. If they suspect a rip-off, blood will flow.

Once the program was designed, it was offered to every member of NOLA on a volunteer basis. Basically, Helton advised everybody "we've got some real high-tech, sexy, sporty things that we can do, but it's up to you to take part." Things, he claims, that are in the AIOs',

Tactical team training begins at dawn with strenuous physical exercises.

Tactical team shooters with coaches run the first of three proficiency courses at the firing range. The shooters are allowed two twelve-round magazines for seventeen targets.

but not the pilots', job description "to keep on top of takedown techniques." In any case, both can participate if they sign up. "So, we wrote the book on aircraft takedown techniques and called it *The Felony Guide To Take Down Suspect Aircraft*."

Interestingly enough, 1,000 miles away at the Tucson Air Branch in Arizona, AIO Bill Dreeland was doing the same thing, as were others in Miami and at the other branches. These plans and proposed programs were directed to Headquarters CNAC, the Customs National Aviation Center, which acknowledged the need for uniform, SWAT-like training. That program, as this book is being written, is undergoing standardization for all aviation branches and units.

Mandatory tactical team refresher training at NOLA is conducted once a month. Advanced training with the latest techniques continues, on a volunteer basis, once a week.

The techniques and tactics taught at NOLA are very similar to those employed by military special forces teams. The only exception is no

"recon by fire." In other words, "don't go out shooting" because unlike a military unit operating in a known hostile environment, Customs has to sort the bad guys from the good guys and any innocent bystanders. These techniques are designed to give Customs aircrews an edge during personal apprehensions while protecting themselves and others.

"Much of our training is for the worst-case scenario, and we need to know when to be prepared to apply our SWAT training and when not to," says Helton. "Would a private pilot," he asks, "of a C-172 who 'blew off' the ADIZ, actually fire two rounds [after landing] and run into the woods just to avoid talking to a law enforcement officer because he made a mistake? Hell no! He might be angry that he got caught and stopped, and he might be belligerent but, is he in need of prone cuffing and compliance techniques resulting in a hard takedown? Hell no! He's a private citizen that screwed up!"

Customs admits to cases where personnel have been overzealous with a legitimate pilot who might have given them reason to believe his actions fit a smuggler's profile, but those are not the norm. Usually they have time and information to sort the good guys from the bad guys. They don't train to avoid legitimate pilot complaints. Legitimate civilian and corporate pilots need to understand that Customs air walks a fine line between the potential for a full-fledged firefight and a routine traffic stop.

Mark confides, "Our biggest fear is the same as the smuggler's biggest fear." Dopers are never confident of who or what they are up against and are ready to engage anyone who may rip them off—in a heartbeat! A Customs interdiction does not pose near the threat to a doper, that getting ripped off by a rival smuggler or drug dealer does. They know that shooting at a law enforcement officer carries greater legal penalties than those for drug smuggling. But, bear in mind that the bad guys don't know if or when it's a Customs takedown and may begin shooting to kill before the badges are flashed!

The bottom line is that Customs trains for a worst-case scenario involving potential life and death situations.

Tactical Team Training

The exercises, run by Mark Helton and Jim Esposito, are full of mock SWAT scenarios. The day begins with strenuous runs, rope climbing and obstacle courses. It continues with aircraft takedown and assault techniques and ends, late in the afternoon, with combat shoots and static handcuffing drills.

It is hot and muggy—a typical 90 percent humidity, ninety-degree day at the firing range. Each tactical team member has two twelve-round magazines for the first course: one in the gun and one on the table. Two shooters, each with his respective coach, run the course together. All seventeen targets on the first course are stills; square metal targets on posts, black and white posters of bad guys shooting back and small round metal disks on the grass.

"Shooters ready? Coaches ready? Shooters stand by. Snap on. Commence!" The two-person teams run twenty yards on a circular course to the first target and the sharp unmistakable cracks and echoes of pistol shots pierce the air. They stop, aim, shoot, then run along a parallel line across eight targets, three yards apart, ten and twenty yards away. They reload their weapons and continue. Having finished the exercise, they unload the weapon and hold it up in one hand, the magazine in the other.

When all the tactical team members have run the first course, they proceed to the second: sixteen targets with two twelve-round magazines, one in the gun, one on the table. Some of the targets are moving targets and some require covered positions crouching behind objects commonly found on a street, like mailboxes.

After completing the second event, they run a third course, all while simulating an incapacitating hit or injury resulting in a weak or disabled arm, forcing them to kneel down to reload their weapon with the weak hand. If they are right-handed they have to use their left hand and vice versa. The object is to fire twelve rounds, reload the magazine, insert it into the gun, chamber a round and fire twelve more rounds—weak hand only.

The remainder of the day is taken up with dynamic stacking, cuffing and takedown exer-

The third and last firing event simulates an incapacitating hit or injury to the gun hand where the shooter fires twelve rounds, reloads the magazine, inserts it into the gun, chambers it and fires twelve more rounds with his weak hand. Two coaches look over the shooter's shoulder.

Tactical team members from NOLA move rapidly on a smuggler aircraft. Experience has taught them that the window of opportunity for a successful takedown, from exiting the Black Hawk to prone cuffing, is ninety seconds.

49

Bust crew members are protected from incoming hostile fire by aircraft surfaces such as wing tips and stabilizers. Their backs are protected by team members who maintain those fields of fire.

cises where they all take turns being the bad guy. When the Louisiana sun begins to reach for the western horizon, the team members of the New Orleans Aviation Branch sit down to clean their weapons and talk about the training before heading back. Some of them go home. Others prepare for the graveyard shift. A few head to the NAS New Orleans officers club or casual bar to rehash events and lessons and wash down the day with hairy tales about the "guy that didn't get away."

Evolving Role in Interdiction

As the Customs aviation role evolves, they find themselves more and more in a law enforcement support role. In Louisiana, border land seizures in 1990 were up 600 percent. Those figures are indicative that the Customs air impact has forced the "low-flying, multi-engined junkie with high-tech electronics who risked flying the Gulf at night" to shift his tactics to maritime and overland modes of transportation.

Land operations require close coordination with local law enforcement agencies. Often, when sufficient time is allowed, NOLA officers will support local and regional law enforcement operations. Say, for instance, they have information on an air drop that's going down in three hours, on the same afternoon they have committed to supporting a local DEA operation involving a meth (methane, or crack-producing) lab. The normal aircrews on duty will handle the air intercept while a special tactical team will be put together for the DEA operation.

Not long ago, one such operation was directed, not against a crack house, but against a "crack street" in a New Orleans shrimper community. A local law enforcement task force had requested NOLA to provide "a distraction for execution of warrants obtained for crack suspects." DEA wanted to lure the bad guys out and grab them, while people on the street would be distracted by something else.

The Customs Black Hawk was singled out as the most powerful tool for distraction available in the Customs inventory, particularly because it was loaded with a bust team in the event the bad guys would have runners that tried to get away.

The pilot of the Hawk was instructed to make a low-altitude, high-speed flight down the middle of this crack street while simultaneously, the local police arrived in vehicles! As it turned out, the suspects were indeed standing out on the street, looking skyward, stunned by the Hawk as the cops bailed out of their cars and headed towards them. The result was phenomenal. Even as the bad guys were being handcuffed, they *continued* to look up with no resistance! More than twenty suspects were arrested and a large amount of crack seized with no injuries to anyone. The only real surprise was later that night when business on the street returned as usual!

Tactical Scenario

A suspect airplane has been intercepted by a NOLA Citation, followed down by the matte-black painted Hawk whose pilot has positioned himself at a forty-five-degree angle, twenty yards off the target's nose in a ninety-degree position to the smuggler aircraft. All Hawk aircrews are in full BDU (battle dress uniform) and combat gear—weapons, bulletproof vests, survival gear, helmets, radios and cuffs. As a measure of pride they wear the team's black T-shirt imprinted with a yellow star, superimposed with a Black Hawk and the words "New Orleans Special Helicopter Interdiction Team." The capital letters spell out NOSHIT.

By the time the Hawk is in position and stabilized, they have unbuckled their waist and shoulder harnesses. Weapons have been checked and readied for a head-on deployment. Each team member knows what his or her field of fire is going to be.

The team doesn't always know how the pilot is going to land, but the ideal situation, from their backseat standpoint, is a six o'clock deployment from the chopper. That should put the team in a ninety-degree position to port (door side) of the smuggler plane. In the dynamic stacking order the only team member that is briefly exposed to gunfire is the TTL, the tactical team leader, who has to assess the security position of his team.

Whether it's a left or right single-door egress from the Hawk, the TTL will be in the gunner's position. The six-person team deploys from the Hawk in dynamic stacking order: TTL first, Contact Man, Arrest One, Arrest Two, Security One, and Security Two last. Ideal conditions at night are for the team to egress on the same side as the chopper's night sun where they have a blinding advantage. Security Two opens the door and calls, "Clear." The TTL calls, "Deploy! Deploy! Deploy!" and goes out first while training his weapon on the smuggler aircraft.

They line up in close single file, guns down, heads low (the blades are still turning), hugging the helo, left hand on the shoulder of the person in front, right hand holding their long weapons down to the "rally point."

Security Two closes the door, squeezes Security One's shoulder, who passes the silent signal forward. It serves two purposes, a "ready, set" sign to all members, and to the TTL whose back is to his crew. Remember, if it's a night bust, the only thing they can see without NVGs (Night

The NOLA Bayou Bushwackers patch.

Vision Goggles, which also limit their field of vision) is what they can feel.

Thirty seconds after they have deployed from the Hawk, the "window of operation for a successful bust" is ninety seconds to get into place, determine how many people are in the aircraft, get them out and take them down.

They run towards the port side of the aircraft and maintain a field of fire which exposes the smuggler aircrews and ground load crews to everything they've got. That serves as a deterrent to keep the suspects from shooting or running. "That much more reason to bear down, make eye contact and show 'em what we've got," says Mark Helton. They assume strategic defensive and assault positions around the aircraft which gives them a clear field of fire to any target plus protection from a smuggler's gunsight.

Two minutes later, three suspects—two pilots and a suspect on the ground who tried to run—are face down, spread-eagled on the tarmac and cuffed as the TTL reads them their rights.

Three hundred and fifty kilos of cocaine are seized. Street value $8,755,000.

Chapter 6

The Attitude

All Customs men and women in aviation operations are a special breed. They are warriors. They are risk takers. And, like any individual in any high-risk profession—fighter pilots, firefighters, race-car drivers and others—they are highly trained, well equipped and have the right attitude, "the right stuff." It is a quality that can best be described by the following famous, but anonymous, epilogue about fighter pilots: "Fighter Pilots Do It Better."

The fighter pilot has certain characteristics which give him a distinct individual identity. The ideal fighter pilot puts his all into everything he does. He has a can-do attitude. He displays enthusiasm and instills this feeling in those about him. The fighter pilot believes the job should be done the right way and only one time, the first time. He tries hard to be the very best at everything he does. He expects others to do the same. The fighter pilot tries to be an expert in his field, always seeking new knowledge and experience. He tries to broaden his experience by not confining himself to one narrow channel. The fighter pilot believes in himself. He has a tremendous amount of pride in himself and in everything that he does. He works hard and plays hard; always a competitor in both, to the very best of his ability. When he discovers a problem he always comes up with an answer. He respects those who have earned respect. He is more than willing to help those who need help.

Do fighter pilots do it better? Yes, they do everything better! But nowhere above does it state that fighter pilots fly aircraft or engage in aerial combat. You don't even have to fly to be characterized a fighter pilot. A fighter pilot is more than a flyer. A fighter pilot is an attitude, and people with that attitude, no matter what their station in life or their job, really do it better.

Training for the Customs Mission

Qualifications for becoming a member of the Customs Aviation Program are not easy to meet. To begin with, extensive background checks are made on all individuals prior to an entrance exam. Typically, 500 people competing for available AIO slots will be tested over five days. Out of those, only fourteen to twenty will be hired. Pilot slots are even harder to come by. Pilots are really selected for their flying skills, rather than hired for their profession.

Although air interdiction is the primary mission for Customs aviation, their secondary function is mission support to law enforcement agencies. Once the new-hires go through primary Customs law enforcement orientation, Customs air may lose a few individuals to other Customs divisions such as Fraud, Child Pornography, Exodus (illegal exportation of goods and services), Border Exit and Entry, and others.

All Customs aviation new-hires, whether they be pilots or air interdiction officers, attend a four-month school at the Federal Law Enforcement Training Center (FLETC). The school is divided into two sections, a criminal investigation school involving Federal laws and Federal jurisdiction process in the United States, followed by a school on Customs enforcement and border-search authority.

Further mandatory courses involve instruction at NAS Corpus Christi on the F-16 radar and FLIR system, where the AIOs also receive basic aviation ground school and ten hours of flight school. Upon completion of the above, all aircrews are put through the altitude chamber, egress training and water survival at NAS Pensacola or NAS Jacksonville. Here they get qualified in the underwater helicopter dunker where they learn to survive a crash, use PLFs (personal life equipment) and underwater breathing devices.

Unique to the Customs Aviation Program, prior to 1988, was an additional three-week aviation enforcement course given at Marana Air Base in Arizona. Instruction at Marana for all new-hires would include courses on reconnaissance, surveillance, installation of law enforcement transponders and tracking devices, special assault techniques and self-defense. Since those courses are no longer available, Customs air personnel conduct in-depth, in-house training specific to those areas. Additionally, all aircrews maintain up-to-date qualifications on sensor software and hardware upgrades, ground tactics, mapping, ground school, weapons training, water survival refresher courses, self-defense and assault techniques.

Both pilots and AIOs are hired under the Customs 18-11 title series for Customs officers. The pilots fall under a GS 21-81 category specifying primary aviator responsibilities; the AIOs fall under GS 1884-9/11 for criminal investigators with primary responsibilities as airborne sensor systems operators. This function also requires a thorough knowledge of undercover work. Often, the demand for a Customs AIO agent to do undercover work will be prompted by a lack of electronic signals and human intelligence in the field, particularly in large geographic areas like the southwest and the Gulf coast.

Women Warriors

Women in Customs aviation make up about 8 percent of the force and are still an oddity. Few and far between, the women, like their military counterparts, work as equal partners with the men. They perform the same job functions as male Customs pilots and AIOs, receive the same training, work the same cases, have the same qualifications and share equally in the glory and defeat of the Customs interdiction mission.

Lori's Story

At twenty-five years of age, Lori Janosko, Customs criminal investigator and AIO, is one of the few women in the aviation program and even fewer women in the New Orleans Aviation Branch. "I joined the branch directly from college, in 1987," says Janosko. "Having majored in law and having a hankering for criminal justice," she took the Treasury Enforcement Agent Exam, "and the next thing I knew, I was offered a job."

Lori was surprised to find that she was the first and only female (at that time) to be hired as an aircrew member by NOLA. "I quickly realized that I was entering a male-dominated domain," but claims she was not in the least daunted by the proposition. Since that time, the branch has hired two other female AIOs for a total of three; a number which is fairly representative of Customs aviation branches and units.

Janosko learned how to run the sensor equipment prior to the formal training now offered to AIOs and has since become a radar instructor. "After a two-week basic course on technical-capability aspects of the radar, and on the software packages designed for air intercepts," she explained, "training was a 'hands-on' process involving a series of flights." Running the radar is really "the best way to learn. This area of the Gulf is always busy with single-engined 'fish spotters' (especially during shrimping season) and military helicopters on training sorties. Both make good target practice." Within two months of flying sensor missions, the NOLA AIO said she was comfortable with her capabilities.

Other AIO duties involve surveillance, intelligence gathering and investigation on major drug smuggling cases, all of which require paperwork. All cases are documented in hard-copy statements which, upon completion, are handed over to a Customs special agent at the OE (Office of Enforcement) or to a US Attorney for prosecution.

At NOLA, the AIO TTL is normally charged with the chain of evidence and the paperwork resulting from a bust. "This branch is very supportive in allowing all the air interdiction officers to go out and do their own investigation on a case," claims Janosko. "We're not just 'scope dopes', we're criminal investigators." The TTL also insures that each team member has a hand-held radio, that he or she is briefed on the proposed operation, is fully equipped and qualified for the operation and is carrying the right weapons.

This female AIO (like all AIOs) is qualified to carry 9 mm and .357 magnum revolvers and 5.56 mm NATO Steyr AUG (Army Universal Gewehr) semiautomatic assault rifles. "Because we basically operate on cold hits," said Janosko, on all missions the aircrews are required to carry a standard sidearm weapon and a back-up weapon. "I normally carry the 9 mm and, depending on what I'm wearing, I'll strap a back-up gun to my ankle or carry it in a flightsuit pocket," says Janosko. Long guns are required only when they fly in the Black Hawk, the favorite weapon being the AUG.

Standard issue handguns for Customs aircrews are Smith & Wesson Model 6906 9 mm double action, semiauto pistols; Smith & Wesson .357 magnum revolvers; and .38-caliber Smith & Wesson Chiefs Special (Model 60) revolvers. The standard long gun is the AUG, and the standard issue shotgun is a 12-gauge Remington Model 870 pump.

Other weapons preferred by Customs pilots and AIOs are Heckler & Koch Model 33KA3

All Customs men and women in aviation operations are highly trained, well-equipped and professional warriors.

rifles in 5.56 mm NATO, Smith & Wesson Model 686 three-inch barrel revolvers, M-16 rifles and 9 mm Walther PPK pistols. When they are not being worn, they are kept in weapons storage lockers, cleaned, oiled and ready for immediate use.

Customs aircrews must meet firearms qualifications every three months. Little leeway is alloted in this policy and those who don't qualify will be looking for a new job.

Sharpshooter

Joan "Corky" Hamilton, an AIO assigned to the Miami Aviation Branch, is a firearms instructor and a member of the Black Hawk bust crew. Her career in law enforcement began in 1978 when she became a public safety officer in Tennessee. In 1983 she was hired as a firearms instructor at FLETC and distinguished herself by becoming the first woman ever to earn a

Joan "Corky" Hamilton served with Customs in Key Largo, Florida, as a criminal investigator prior to serving as an AIO and member of the Black Hawk bust team with the Miami Air Branch. Women in Customs aviation work and war as pilots, AIOs, agents and criminal investigators. They are equal partners with their male counterparts and share in both the glory and defeat of the Customs air interdiction mission. Miami Air Branch

position on the Customs National Pistol Team. In 1985, she earned the title of the NRA National Police Revolver Women's Champion which led her to compete and win five gold medals at the World Police Olympics in 1986.

Corky's continuing achievements in law enforcement in general, and Customs in particular, have made an impressive mark for women in these fields. In 1989, she won the Police Revolver Championship and "High Woman." Later that year, after competing against 350 of the world's best shooters, she earned international recognition by winning ten gold medals and two bronze medals at the International Law Enforcement Olympics in Australia. (Corky Hamilton has since joined the US Forest Service.)

Bust Crews

For a long time, Corky Hamilton and comrade Vickie Edwards were the only female AIOs on the Miami Air Branch bust crew. Being a Customs officer "can get exciting," admitted Edwards, who used to be a Panama Canal Zone police officer, "until Jimmy Carter gave away the canal and my job." When Vickie first joined Customs in 1986, it was with the Marine Division where she drove a cigarette boat on surface interdiction missions against other go-fasts and smuggler vessels. Clad in "proper Florida gear," looking much like "two gals out for some fun 'n sun," she and her female partner caught many a wide-eyed, unbelieving doper who, even after being cuffed, did not believe the two were Customs agents!

Since joining the air branch, Edwards has also become a radar instructor. When a new-hire joins the ranks at Miami, she is one of the people who teaches him or her "the real ropes" in a two-week, in-house sensor course involving serious and sometimes dangerous "yanking and banking" aboard the Citation.

Air interdiction is a lethal role, most often played at night under risky, unpredictable conditions. Many missions take place in dark skies against unseen targets where all aircraft fly without navigation or anticollision lights. They are low-altitude flights, requiring maximum performance and complicated aerial maneuvers to safely intercept, track and bust the smuggler aircraft and its occupants. Training for effective teamwork and accurate communications between aircrew members can make the difference between success and tragedy.

There are other women in Customs aviation, pilots as well as AIOs, whose achievements should be heralded along with their male partners in this book. They are women who epitomize the fighter-pilot attitude with outstanding professional backgrounds ranging from SWAT teams and special operations forces to test pilots. These female Customs officers either preferred not to be singled out for their performance and experience standards, or were presently involved in undercover work. Some of those officers are assigned to the Tucson Air Branch in Arizona and the Riverside Unit in California.

Riverside Air Unit

About a stone's throw from Air Ops West, C3I at March AFB is a modest but secure facility housing the Customs Riverside Air Unit. Dick Roberts, aviation supervisor, claims the unit is "unique, a bit independent, but unique." Officially formed in 1985 under the San Diego Aviation Branch, the Riverside Unit comes under the command of Stan Adams, a Navy-trained P-3 pilot who is the branch chief at San Diego.

Roberts is also a former Navy pilot. However, after flying A-4s and being honorably discharged from the service, he swore if he ever flew again it was "going to be with a glass in my hand, at the rear of an airplane!" True to his feelings at the time, he promptly became a law enforcement officer with the San Bernadino Police Department. "Best damn job I ever had!" he claims. "Why I ever left I don't know, if I had it to do all over again, I'd still be pushing a motorcycle." Somehow, one does not quite believe him for, in the rare combination of past law enforcement and aviation careers, he has brought a wealth of knowledge and experience to the Riverside Unit, where he continues to fly—sans a glass in his hand.

"Customs air" says the supervisor, "is unique in the war on drugs in that we support many state and local agencies with assets they don't have. Our C-210 and our Jet Ranger are used almost daily in assisting the local OE [Customs Office of Enforcement] in narcotics busts, surveillance, top cover, medevac, etc. We use the King Air for normal daytime intercepts and the two Hawks for busts. We get calls from all and respond to all, to the point where we are part of the local law enforcement departments."

DEA Aviation

Formerly under US Customs Service, known as BNDD (Bureau Narcotics Drug Department), the DEA (Drug Enforcement Administration) was formed in 1973 with primary responsibility for ground interdiction, enforcement, forfeiture and support investigations.

Corky Hamilton was the undisputed champion of the 1989 World Police Olympics where she was awarded ten gold medals and two bronze medals. A Customs firearms instructor, Hamilton began a law enforcement career in 1978 as a public safety officer with the Tennessee Valley Authority in Knoxville. Miami Air Branch

The reorganization and creation of the DEA as a "superagency" paved the way for transfers of 500 Customs agents to the new organization, and internalized ongoing turf and drug-war rivalries between the CIA, BNDD, FBI, Customs and now, DEA. Political efforts, over the next ten years, to quell inter-agency bickering would be fruitless and in fact, add fuel to the fires. In 1981 a senior FBI official, Francis Mullen, was appointed as the top DEA administrator and from that point on DEA was owned—lock, stock and barrel—by the FBI.

Today, DEA warriors can be found in every town and city across the United States and in over forty countries across the globe.

Flying a mixed variety of fixed-wing and rotary aircraft, their aviation unit is primarily charged with drug activity surveillance, erradication, suppression and mission support. In 1990, the unit flew 432 DCE/SP (Domestic Cannabis Erradication/Suppression Program) missions and charged the Civil Air Patrol (CAP) with 545 DCE/SP missions in thirty states. According to the DEA, CAP was responsible for the destruction of 40,244 "ditchweed" and 156,646 cultivated plants.

Reported DEA statistics for DCE/SP in 1990 were 5,729 arrests, 38,691,584 assets and 7,328,769 cultivated plants. The state of California led in the arrest and assets numbers and Missouri led in cultivated plants.

Forfeiture and Seizure Laws

Roberts explains how DEA works with Customs: "Although DEA uses surveillance aircraft for investigative and surveillance purposes, Customs still maintains border integrity and are the primary investigative body. Initially, when DEA was formed, we lost a lot of Customs agents, who still had border search authority, to DEA. But, as those people retired, DEA lost that authority [it was not a requirement for new-hires] and it created a problem for both agencies.

"Under new laws," he explained, "when Customs got a load of dope, they'd have to call DEA who would often take four to five hours to get out to the bust site to take jurisdiction over the dope, the arrest and control of the aircraft.

This got tiresome. Customs was very efficient at what they were doing in the late seventies, even though they did not have high-tech sensor birds. It got to the point where DEA would confidently say 'you handle it, you do the report, give us a copy of the report and we'll turn it over to the US Attorney.'"

As this practice became the rule, it became easier for Customs to hand over the narcotics to DEA after directly handling the busts and the paperwork. So, DEA and Customs both used the seizure authority [previously maintained by the US Attorney's Office] under a new law; Title 21-881. In effect, the new forfeiture law read, "To stop the drug trade, you may seize the assets that were purchased or financed by proceeds of drug trafficking."

Roberts claims "881 was a godsend because the suspect had to prove what you [the agent] said was not true rather than [the agent] saying it was true. It was a great law and was the easiest authority to prove seizures! It became damn near impossible for the bad guys to get around them."

In other words, when property is seized it becomes a civil case as opposed to a criminal case. Those laws specify that inanimate objects cannot commit a crime, and "you can't take dope, airplanes, etc. to jail," Roberts said. "You seize them. Then, the case and the property become a civil matter. Unlike criminal laws, civil laws state that the suspect has to prove that the evidence against him is false rather than the agent proving that the evidence is true."

Unfortunately, 881 developed some drawbacks that emerged in the 1980s. DEA became possessive of the law at a political level, which resulted in cross-claiming assets seized by Customs. "DEA would lay claim to 'this seizure or that seizure,'" remarked Roberts, "and they would end up getting all the Congressional money because Customs, even though we were the prosecutors, was giving DEA all the dope!" Nonetheless he adds, "Customs worked well with local DEA RAC and SAC [Resident and Special Agents in Charge] offices whose agents were willing to say 'there's enough for all,' so our operations really did not change." It was also agreed that Customs could keep its own seizure fund under Title 21 "and not hand it all over to DEA," he added, "to which the US Attorney in D.C. agreed."

However, after Customs Commissioner Von Raab relinquished 881 jurisdiction in 1989 to DEA (much to the field's dismay and anguish), US Customs Service implemented Title 49-1472. A new law, designed to assist aircraft seizures from smugglers, it was not as broad as 881. Under the new directive, both Customs and DEA have a similar seizure statue, but "for a Customs agent to continue use of Title 21 authority, he or she has to be cross-designated by DEA authority," Roberts explained. "And, for the whole West Coast, there are only 400 out of 1,000 [nationwide] Customs cross-designated agents!

"When 881 went down the drain for Customs, we lost a lot. We lost a good law . . . and, we lost a lot of airplanes we could have seized because we are not all cross-designated. Only certain select agents, under Title 21 authority, are cross-designated. Moreover, none of my people are, and chances of them getting it, are closer to none than slim.

"Luckily," he continued, "we have a very good relationship with local Customs Office of Enforcement. I came from that office to air and their boss went from air to OE. We understand each other's problems. Nevertheless, he has certain rules that he has to follow and has to say 'I can't cross-designate you.' So, we do all the paperwork on a seizure, advise Customs OE and they send out a cross-designated agent who looks over everything and seizes it.

"If you look at Customs seizure statistics after 1472 was implemented . . . say, '89 stats compared to '90 stats . . . the difference is millions and millions of dollars less for Customs. We could make up total Customs differences with a good year in other departments for money laundering, money seizures, duties and regulatory stuff but, when it came to narcotics, we really got hurt!

"The bottom line," says the unit supervisor, "is that next year, when substantial Customs aviation assets are reflected in the Customs seizure fund, DEA will claim the same assets.

Even though the seizure was made by Customs, it's a DEA stat and that info goes before Congress for future funding."

A No-Win Situation

Customs Air, as a deterrent force to the airborne drug hunter, has to maintain a ready bullet. However, the Riverside Unit Supervisor claims that Customs air intercept has been so efficient that they have almost put themselves out of business. As discussed in previous chapters, smugglers are not crossing the border the way they used to. They are air-dropping, landing across the border, building tunnels, using mule trains, eighteen-wheelers, submarines and getting the dope across any way they can.

"Occasionally," says Roberts, "we get an airplane. About one every five to six months, whereas back in 1986, I personally seized twelve airplanes in one year. Since then, it's been a gradual decline."

Successful air interdiction in California since 1986, forced the dopers to switch tactics. The first year, they would land in the deserts

Air Group Supervisor Dick Roberts (fourth from the left), and aircrews pose in dress blues at Riverside. Riverside Air Unit

59

The Riverside Air Unit patch.

and dry lake beds. A year later, they began landing blatantly at the airports. In 1988, they turned to renting hangars, pulling into them and quickly closing the doors which would cause Customs officers to "lose visual sight" and therefore "legally protect" the traffickers. In 1989, Customs was forced to secure search warrants for those hangars, if and when they could prove that a smuggler was *seen* crossing the border illegally. Otherwise, they couldn't go in after him!

As a result, the Riverside supervisor says, "we started hitting the airports, taking down tail numbers, developing sources of information and setting up surveillance based on all that information. Then, when the airplane landed, we wouldn't let him taxi to the hangar. We had a 'visual' on him and nailed the guy right there. That was legal."

Recently, in February 1991, Riverside had a classic report of a night air drop into the Colorado River. The guy came up from Mexico, followed the river to Lake Havasu, in Arizona, made the drop, did a 180 and headed back south again. The bundles were lit up with glow sticks, the bad guys came out with boats and picked up the load while San Diego Chets and Riverside Black Hawks were en route. "We couldn't get there fast enough so we called ahead and got the local P.D.," Roberts commented, "and they came roaring down the road, lights flashing. By the time the bad guys had docked, law enforcement searches revealed that the boats were clean."

The smugglers had probably sunk the dope with rocks, ridding themselves of incriminating evidence while the plane hightailed it back to Mexican airspace. All of them got off scot-free.

Customs strategy demands that a sensor bird or other aircraft be constantly patrolling the border. And, unless they have good intel, full-time ground and air surveillance is not justified. Both those types of surveillance are cost prohibitive. For this reason, CAP (among other non-Customs assets) is used for long-range reconnaissance operations. Furthermore, as anyone who has seen a Black Hawk or Citation knows, you can't fly those aircraft without that mission being classified as high visibility!

Part II—Scope Warriors

Chapter 7

NORAD

The North American Aerospace Defense Command, NORAD, is a US-Canadian command charged with safeguarding the airspace of the United States and Canada. Via sensors around the world, NORAD can tell if an attack on North American air or space is imminent and if so, national command authorities in both countries are advised for decisions on response. That complicated but fine-tuned process, from initial detection to threat assessment and missile warning provision, takes four minutes to achieve.

Four of the five US commands involved in the anti-drug effort are:
(1) CINCPAC, Commander In Chief Pacific, with defense responsibility for the Pacific Ocean regions
(2) CINCLANT, Commander In Chief Atlantic, CINCPAC's counterpart in the Atlantic regions
(3) CINCSOUTH, Commander In Chief South, with defense responsibility for the Panama Canal, Caribbean and Gulf waters and US territories in those regions
(4) CINCNORAD, Commander In Chief NORAD, whose aerial defense responsibilities are all coastal areas of the North American Air Defense Identification Zone (ADIZ) which surround the continent
Additionally, a newer fifth Command, CINCFOR or Commander In Chief Forces, has

been given land defense responsibility for the Continental United States (CONUS).

Headquartered at Peterson AFB and Cheyenne Mountain AFB in Colorado, NORAD is tasked by the Secretary of Defense to provide assistance to US counternarcotics efforts. Within this framework, NORAD conducts vast detection and monitoring operations of suspect aircraft believed to be smuggling illegal drugs into North America.

Beginning with the 1989 Defense Authorization Act, three joint task forces, belonging to the CINCs, were implemented to assist in the command, control and communications efforts of the war on drugs: Joint Task Force 6 (JTF-6) in Texas under CINCFOR, JTF-5 in California under CINCPAC, and JTF-4 in Florida under CINCLANT. The JTFs are comprised of Army, Navy, Coast Guard, Air Force and Marine personnel.

CINCNORAD's commitment to the counternarcotics program (second only to their warning and assessment mission) is to reduce and eliminate the flow of illegal drugs into North America and to detect and monitor illegal drug traffic.

Command and control operations for federal counternarcotics operations are a natural extension of NORAD's mission. To effectively carry out that responsibility, NORAD integrates the operations of Customs, DEA, Coast Guard, Air National Guard, FAA, Civil Air Patrol and Canadian Defense Headquarters into an efficient and

Defense operation crews at NORAD monitor and sort suspect tracks of airborne smugglers attempting to penetrate the ADIZ (American Air Defense Identification Zone) which surrounds the continental United States.

robust C3I network. Official liaisons from Customs, DEA and the FAA, plus Air National Guard advisors and Coast Guard staff, work directly with NORAD at Peterson AFB.

ADOC

The heart of NORAD's counternarcotic operations takes place at the Air Defense Operations Center, ADOC. Renovated in 1989 and harbored deep in the heart of the Cheyenne Mountain Complex, ADOC is a surprisingly small, low-ceilinged, multi-consoled area that is "sanitized" prior to an outsider's entrance. Myriad classified, secret, top secret and SCI (special compartmented information) information is cleared from the screens. Colored phones on the commander's desk link the command center to ADOC and, with equal billing, to all the Canadian and US national command authorities and anybody else with a need to know. Gray walls and beige carpet soothe the operations crews, who spend eight-hour shifts peering at green monochrome scopes, multi-colored screens and maps. A certain air of intensity is palpable.

Because NORAD's airspace-surveillance system is a decentralized one, only unknown tracks and those of other significance are forwarded by JTF and ROCC (Region Operations Control Centers) to ADOC. The suspected narcotic tracks are referred to as Special 17s designating a high interest, suspected or confirmed counternarcotics track. For quick, visual track and monitoring, the Special 17s are labeled in code according to the information at hand. For instance, Special 17s in pink windows or blocks, are priority targets needing ID or more information. All Special 17s are forwarded to Customs C3Is.

One of the officers who helped set up this dynamic counternarcotics system for NORAD is Maj. John Conkel. Overseeing all ADOC operations, he explains, "Basically, we can eliminate all scope tracks displaying speeds in excess of 180 knots. Out of those remaining, the ones that are not identified, or meet a smuggler's profile, become our Special 17s. In [fiscal year] 1990 we had 317 confirmed [by prior intel] Special 17s and a total of 1,015 unconfirmed. Every one of them was intercepted, identified, tracked and monitored. Those that landed in the US were busted."

Interestingly enough, one of the things that NORAD learned in the initial stages of setting up a joint network with so many law enforcement agencies, was the necessity of having to learn each other's operational language, acronyms and classifications.

The language problem was quickly dealt with. However, the classification problem was not so easy. What DEA (under the Department of Justice) considered classified information, material or assets, differed somewhat from what the CINCs (under DoD) considered classified and vice versa. The same held true of Customs (under the Department of Treasury) and Coast Guard (under the Department of Transportation), NORAD, the FBI and others. All those differences, however minor, had to be ironed out. Furthermore, operational and responsibility problems and complaints, caused by a failure to read off the same sheet of music, emerged and prevail today.

Nationally, there are somewhere between 300 and 350 organizations connected with narcotics at local, state and national levels. Even though they share the same objective, to get all of them moving in harmony, in the same direction, has been a feat of significant proportions. However, Major Conkel confidently claims, "NORAD and the war on drugs is 100 percent ahead of where it was two and three years ago." And, when all of various factions in this complicated and intricate network do operate together and effectively, the following is what happens.

NORAD-Assisted Busts

While working on a narcotics case in Canada, the Royal Canadian Mounted Police (RCMP) received a tip-off that a known, watched and wanted bad guy had launched out of Colombia and was headed their way in an Aero Commander. NORAD monitored the northbound track, allowed the smuggler to "roll" through the Caribbean, the ADIZ and up the northeast coast of the United States. At 0639 hours local, a prepositioned NORAD E-3 AWACS, off of New Hampshire, detected a target at 1,000 feet that fit the description. At 0700, the E-3 controller handed him off to a waiting Customs P-3 who established loose trail. Customs then launched a Cheyenne from Bangor, Maine, that intercepted the aircraft at 0741, visually identified it and continued tracking it. At 0806 the bad guys landed, with a certain amount of audacity, on an airfield they had bought in Weyman, New Brunswick. The alerted and ready Mounties nailed the aircraft, seized the drugs and arrested the two pilots. Approximately 1,100 pounds of cocaine were confiscated and two pilots were sentenced to twenty-two years in prison.

The story doesn't end here; it gets better. One of the pilots, whose last name was Escobar (strong evidence shows that he may have been related to infamous drug kingpin, Pablo Escobar), became a "prime take out" target for two different Colombian hit squads. Prior intel alerted law enforcement authorities to the planned hits. Both attempts were allowed but foiled and eventually, the success of this particu-

The entrance to NORAD's ADOC (Air Defense Operations Center) in the Cheyenne Mountain complex is guarded by massive blast doors with a swing weight of thirty tons each which can be opened or closed in forty-five seconds. NORAD

Customs aircraft meet with other adversaries besides smuggler aircraft. This Cuban MiG-21 was photographed by a Miami Air Branch pilot who was, in no uncertain terms, advised to stay clear of Cuban airspace. Miami Air Branch

lar case led Customs and the RCMP to twenty-five subsequent arrests.

On another night, NORAD observed an airplane take off out of Hermosillo, Mexico, and fly up into California. They alerted C3I and several Customs interceptors were launched. Somehow, the smugglers realized they had been intercepted and made (the only right move all night) a quick and dirty 180-degree turn back to the border, where they loitered on the Mexican side. Foolishly thinking they were in the clear, the guys flew back across the Arizona border (penetrating a US military restricted area) and doggedly headed north again, this time towards Sedona, Arizona. (It was later determined that Sedona was their original destination.)

Not sure if their frequencies were being monitored by Customs, the smugglers radioed waiting ground load crews that they "might be tailed." The ground crews replied, "We're outta here," and were never seen or heard from again. Well, that must have ticked off the pilots because they still had a load of dope to deliver if they

The controllers at ADOC monitor tracks detected by NORAD specialists or forwarded to NORAD by other DoD surveillance centers. These Special 17 tracks designate high-interest, suspected or confirmed narcotics targets which can be forwarded to C3I for intercept action. NORAD

were going to get paid and worse yet, they were running low on fuel. They did another 180, flew south to Cottonwood and touched down on that runway only to be greeted by eleven waiting Customs aircraft, among them two Black Hawks! The dopers quickly added power, got airborne and attempted to escape. However, they were followed in close trail by Customs aircraft, nearly blinded by the Hawk's night sun and forced to land again. The pilots turned out to be first-time rookies, two commercial airline pilots who had been lured into risking "one or two quick runs" by "quick and substantial payoffs."

Over-The-Horizon Radar

A little-known radar, the Over-The-Horizon Backscatter, OTH-B, has been around for twelve or thirteen years. However, it has also been the focus of bureaucratic budget bickering.

Primarily designed as a strategic warning system against Soviet bombers and cruise missiles, the OTH-B also has the capability of accurately picking up small, slow- and low-flying aircraft, 500 to 1,800 miles away from North America.

NORAD's air defense strength lies in mid- to high-altitude threat detection. If it weren't for Customs Aerostats and C3Is, DoD radars and Sector Operational Control Centers (SOCCs), and FAA conventional line-of-sight radars, all of which have gaps, holes and soft spots in their radar coverage, NORAD would have very little low-altitude surveillance capabilities. The OTH-B, presently being tested and evaluated by the Air Force, would provide NORAD with an all-altitude air-threat detection capability. Testing of the OTH-B's coverage in areas south of US borders has proven to be excellent despite the fact that the radar is adversely affected at times by certain atmospheric and ionospheric conditions.

NORAD claims they need four OTH-Bs guarding the eastern, western, southern and northern approaches to North America. Strangely enough, both the East and West Coast sectors have been funded with congressional monies for usage (maintenance, utilities, staffing and so on) of the OTH-B, yet funds for the actual radars intended on those sites have never been approved. With the fact that no additional JTF-linked radars would be forthcoming to safeguard American skies, many folks believed the OTH-B should be implemented.

Controversial opinions persist from it being a panacea for existing radar surveillance deficiencies, to it being a white elephant. For the last decade, while the OTH-B remained a scapegoat for congressional budget battles, year in and year out, the airborne drug smuggler continued to airdrop and off-load billions of dollars of undetected dope.

To make matters worse, in April 1991, Congress decided to reduce funding on the existing OTH-B to a forty-hour week (nine to five, five days a week), mothball the West Coast OTH-B and put the remaining two sites on an indefinite hold. The OTH-B has become a sacrificial lamb in the US budget.

A Chat with the Director

Maj. Gen. Eric Ian Patrick, Canadian Forces, director of combat operations for NORAD, explains the mission in brief. "Take a bubble from the outskirts of the ADIZ surrounding the US. If a legal airplane moves within that airspace, it belongs to the FAA. If it is a military airplane in the air sovereignty mission, it belongs to NORAD. If it is an inbound, unidentified airplane that penetrates the ADIZ, we go after it for identification. If that plane is a foreign military airplane, we respond accordingly, either escort him back out of the ADIZ or escort him to landing. If it is a civilian plane without a flight plan, we report it to the FAA. If it is an airplane in trouble, we guide him in to land, and if it meets a smuggler's profile we advise Customs air. Remember that Customs has border authority into the country. However, they don't have enough airplanes to cover the periphery of the country so, on the Canadian border, the Royal Canadian Mounted Police are charged with responding to border crossing issues.

"In any case, a suspect drug runner is *not* guilty until positive evidence of lawbreaking is associated with his flight, i.e., he has made an overland or overwater air drop outside of the border or he has illegally entered the twelve-

When a Customs interceptor is launched, NORAD tracks and monitors the mission from start to finish.

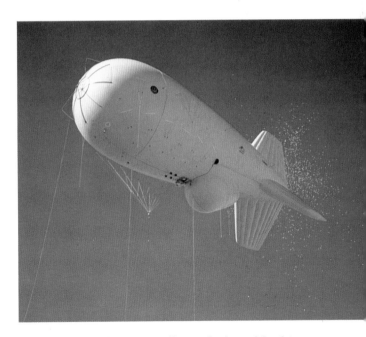

Low-altitude, airborne surveillance platforms like this Customs Aerostat, are simply inadequate to counter the drug threat. The new OTH-B (Over-The-Horizon-Backscatter) radars would give NORAD all-altitude detection capabilities.

A NORAD decal.

with illegal activities appears on the scope, it is tagged by the computer. Let's say this guy suddenly pops up on our scope, flashing a warning code that means air support is required. If he's in the Southwest, Project Alliance kicks into action. From California to Texas, Project Alliance is made up of law enforcement agencies that watch for illegal border crossings and who coordinate their response to that action. North Star is the Canadian counterpart."

Eighty to 90 percent of illegal narcotics that come into North America come in through commercial containers. Even combining efforts with National Guard, Border Patrol and others, Customs officials can only look at 14 percent of the containers that arrive in seaports and airports, and it takes about forty-eight hours to thoroughly search one container! The narcotics traffickers know that and are more than willing to risk 1 percent, a number which can be even lower if the cargo is ingeniously packed and hidden, in order to get the other 86 percent on the streets.

"Those percentages cause 15,000 to 20,000 American deaths every year. The bottom line is that if only 1 percent of the drugs are intercepted, that's 150 to 200 people who may not die drug related deaths. And that is why the drug war is worth the effort."

mile limits of territorial waters or crossed country border lines over land.

"When an American registered aircraft, previously identified by DEA, Customs, etc.,

Chapter 8

C3I

The two Customs C3I (Command, Control, Communications and Intelligence) Centers are the nerve centers of airborne drug interdiction operations in the United States. Both are located in strategic areas, Air Ops East in Miami and Air Ops West in California at March AFB.

C3I provides central direction for Customs air interdiction, using a combined force of Air Force, Navy and Coast Guard sensor and radar aircraft. Linked to CNAC (Customs National Aviation Center), it also combines radar data with intelligence data bases and other ground-air radar systems. Unlike NORAD surveillance radars, Customs' eyes in the sky focus on aircraft flying at 100 to 19,000 feet agl (above ground level) or msl (mean sea level) with speeds of 100 to 350 knots. However, they can look at anything from surface to infinity with speeds in excess of forty knots. Augmented by Aerostats and fourteen-hour endurance Customs P-3 Orions with look-down APS-138 radars, C3I operators can monitor up to 3,000 targets per twelve-second scan and proposed upgrades will soon allow 5,000 targets per twelve-second scan. With these assets, they can effectively track the course of a plane over 3,000 miles and coordinate the interdiction from first detection to the arrest.

The first thing one notices upon entering the confines of C3I West is not the high tech, computerized consoles, monitors and scopes; the first thing one sees, hanging ten o'clock high, ten degrees off the main screens, is a huge, green, eyes-crossed-out alligator with a broken, single-engined plane in its toothy jaws—a gift from C3I in Miami when they heard that C3I West was using CROCC—Customs Radar Operations Control Center—as its logo. Rumor has it that the lifesize, three-dimensional reptile was ripped off from a theater showing *Crocodile Dundee!* The disabled airplane was courtesy of Miami. Standard operating procedure allows for a certain amount of rivalry between Air Ops East and Air Ops West, attributed, in part, to the fact that Miami gets all the money and Air Ops West gets all the dope!

The center's fused information is displayed on nineteen-inch color monitors located in consoles throughout the floor and on two six-by-eight-foot screens on the wall. Practically every airplane in the air (and some on the ground) west of Houston is sorted, good guys from bad guys! Furthermore, watch officers at any of the ten work stations can access any and all radio transmissions this side of VHF, UHV and FM in clear, voice-privacy or encrypted modes. Additionally, each station has access to military Autovon (automatic voice network), FTS (Federal Telephone System), FAA System 300, commercial land lines and government agency "hot lines."

Radar Data and Symbology

Jeff Houlihan, a Customs watch officer and DSS (Detection Systems Specialist) supervisor on the floor, describes the operations. "What you see are eleven different operating positions and two large-screen displays depicting the total area that C3I looks at, and concentrates on. From the Gulf coast to southern California." Everything that a radar can see, assuming all the joint surveillance sites are up and operating, is depicted in that area and repeated at the individual stations. Additionally, each station has two consoles with two mapping and operational intelligence screens each for a total of four screens.

"The operations and intelligence mapping capability side puts us into all the law enforcement computer systems: NCIC [National Center for Intelligence Communications], TECS [Treasury Enforcement Communications System], and PAES [Private Aircraft Enforcement System] which is based on PAIRS [Private Aircraft Inspection Reporting System], etc.," explains Houlihan, "and all of the Customs data bases. It gives us specific information on airports and types of aircraft. It distinguishes those aircraft that we put law enforcement transponders on and tells us where they are."

The other screen depicts surveillance infor-

A C3I controller or watch officer at Air Ops West monitors southwestern border traffic on one of the ten work stations. Should he detect a suspect smuggler, he can relay the information on VHF, UHF and FM clear and secure radio frequencies for appropriate response from aviation branches. C3I West

mation and automated radar data. "It comes in from antenna sites through computer bases into the system," he adds. "So, in essence it is raw radar data that is processed. Every dot or symbol that you see on the screen has a certain amount of information that is associated specifically with that target."

Customs controllers have the capacity to change the range scale on the surveillance screen from one to 3,500 nautical miles. Additionally, the screens designate what kind of airspace the aircraft is operating in—restricted, warning areas, TCAs (Terminal Control Areas) and other airport operating areas. "It makes it considerably easier for us to coordinate our way through those areas while tracking a target," says Houlihan. "For instance, restricted area 2303, here," he points to a section of the Mexico-Arizona border, "marks a spot called J-37 where the Fort Huachuca Aerostat is tethered."

Every piece of symbology on the screen means something. It gives the controller vital information. Green triangles are military aircraft or those squawking Mode 2. Square boxes with a slash mark are "good correlated targets," meaning Customs is receiving a strong radar return off the aircraft or its transponder. Xs are primary targets, pound (#) signs are an indication that the target is beginning to disappear off the screen. A yellow data block means Customs has identified the aircraft via PAIRS records; they know where it's from, where it's going, its time en route and what its estimated time of arrival is. If a controller punches in a select track feature, the computer will bring a map up on the right screen, put an aircraft symbol over that map and show where that aircraft is.

"In the old days," says Houlihan, adding ruefully "and the old days were only a few years ago, we used to pull out sectionals for manual-eyeball, target-terrain reference. Then, we tried to narrow down exactly where that target was. Now, with this system, it allows us to select a large number of types of maps which get into detail. It's unbelievable! Down to the point where you can actually sort and watch an aircraft take off and land."

"IFR"

A common smuggler's ploy, in order to avoid radar detection, is to fly low-level "IFR" ("I follow roads") and lose themselves in ground clutter and traffic. Jeff explains how that aircraft is distinguished from road traffic.

"Let's say I've got an aircraft over a roadway in Mexico—and you can't really tell if it's a plane if he pulls his speed back to match the traffic—but, he can't make the tight highway turns. When he cuts away from the road, we know it's a plane. Even the F-16 radars can't sort that type of a target. We get incredible detail! Right down to city maps, and if the target moves off that map, the system automatically brings up an adjoining map to continue tracking the aircraft."

All types of maps are available at a push of a button; road maps, county maps, sectionals, all

CROCC logo. C3I West

are invaluable in knowing where a target is, where he made the drop (if any) and where to accurately send local law enforcement agencies to make the bust.

Aircraft-specific information on each symbol is shown on the left screen within an associated data block—target heading, altitude, speed, flight-plan information, transponder codes and other pertinent information. For an airplane that is flying without a flight plan or without transponders, Houlihan says, "We get the same type of information with the exception of squawk. Say we have a primary target." He punches a grey button and up comes a screen full of targets. He selects an *X* target. "I run a 'Read Feature' on him." He punches another button on the right screen, "And it tells me that we have no aircraft ID on him. Since he's only a primary, heading southbound right now, he's not a suspect."

Primary refers to limited radar data on a specific target or, as Houlihan puts it, "What you see is what you get!" The computer, for whatever reasons, only tells the controller the track ID, speed, heading, but no altitude. Normally, a primary target is safe or legal traffic. However, they can turn "bad" in a heartbeat!

A Customs P-3B AEW turboprop with a radome mounted on its back has the capacity to search a 200-mile, 360-degree radius. A typical surveillance mission on any P-3 is made up of ten days with two eight-hour flights per day, with two Customs crews plus logistic and maintenance personnel rotating on eight-hour shifts. C3I West

A secondary target is an aircraft with a transponder code. "Let's say we pick up a target in a green box," Houlihan explains. "That is an airplane we have flight plan info on. If I want specific information on who he is, where he came from, type aircraft, etc.," he punches more buttons, "I pull it up on the left console," and *presto,* the computer spits out all that information.

So, what's to keep a smuggler from filing a fake flight plan? Number one, if he doesn't stick to his flight plan, it triggers an investigation. Number two, his times are an indication of his honesty, he only draws attention if they are off, and Customs looks very closely at any deviation from the published flight plan. And number three, a smuggler would only draw attention to himself if he turns off his transponder to simulate a NORDO (no radio) situation. That really raises eyebrows because they suddenly change from secondary and pop up as primary only, immediately becoming a prime suspect.

"Most people," Houlihan confides, "including Air Force, Air National Guard and Navy pilots, don't understand the capabilities we actually have available at our fingertips at C3I. They'll call in what they think is 'a great target,' not knowing that we've been watching the guy since he took off, and know who he is, where he came from and where he is going! It always helps (us and them) when they come in and take a look at the system. Then they know what we are capable of and what we are looking for from them."

Suddenly, a target with a yellow data block emerges on the screen, a PAIRS-identified target. "Let's just watch him to make sure he does what he said he was going to do," the floor supervisor comments, adding "We're not too concerned with the guys that are obviously legal, but we watch them just the same."

Whenever a new target comes up, Customs checks for three things, arrival time, code and heading. First, they check PAIRS to see if the aircraft has an arrival due time. Second, they check to make sure it is transmitting the proper code or an assigned discreet code, ensuring it's flying the right speed for the type of aircraft. "Sometimes they try to fool you," he adds can-

didly. Third, they check what heading it came from and cross-reference that information with his flight path. The yellow-data-block target checked out on all three points. He was OK.

"What you see on a target that is purely suspicious, is this," Houlihan points to an *X,* a primary target on the screen. "When you don't get any other information, like this one, coming up in this direction [the aircraft was in Mexico, heading north] and there is no indication of anybody having filed into Nogales or Tucson, as soon as he touches the border, that's it!" Without having filed legally into one of the ports of entry, or if the aircraft is primary only, Customs scrambles a Citation after him. "Mind you," he says proudly, "these cases are less frequent since the interdiction program has been a deterrent to

The onboard APS-125 radar system with an AYK-14 computer allows Customs P-3B controllers to automatically track a target. Two Miligraphics touch-screen color displays provide visual information on target location, heading, altitude and range. The newer P-3B Orion has an extended range of 4,200 nautical miles with fourteen hours on station. They are equipped with secure data communication systems and advanced APS-138 radar systems which can process more AYK-14 tracks than the APS-125. The price tag on the newer Customs P-3Bs (introduced in 1990) is about $30 million each. C3I West

airborne drug smuggling. We've seen a great trend of change in their tactics."

New Tactics and Strategies

Evolving smuggler's tactics have forced innovative Customs strategies. A couple of years ago, the normal, primary only, aircraft were those that would fly up, land out in the middle of the desert, off-load to a vehicle and then fly into a US airport or back down to Mexico. "The more effective we got," says Houlihan, "the more we began seeing more air drops into the US with the plane doing a 180 and flying back." Even though there are ways of curtailing that action in some cases, the dopers know that Customs aircraft cannot follow them into Mexican airspace. "So, what we tried to do," explains Houlihan, "is take out the load crews and get at least one of them to turn over."

Aerostat radar balloons, designed with a look-down radius aspect, can fill in the radar "holes" left by ground based radars which are line-of-sight restrictive. Once the full Aerostat fence is in place and operational, the total radar coverage will be equivalent to that of twenty-four AEW platforms. C3I West

That strategy could lead to taking out the whole organization and the narcotics traffickers caught on very quickly. They turned to air-dropping a load in a remote area, set a lookout on a mountain and wait for Customs agents to pick up the dope. It became a game of leapfrog. Customs would counter by ignoring the load and putting their own lookout on another mountain to wait for the bad guys to recover the dope. It turned into a waiting game for both sides which led to overland techniques: use of mule trains, building border tunnels, ingesting bags of cocaine and walking across the border, trucking it across, and so on.

"You'd be surprised at how effective we can be with this system on that, too," he grins. "We've made seizures, in conjunction with the Border Patrol where we watched aircraft come up to the border, land on the Mexican side and within minutes take off and head back south. In one case, we notified Border Patrol plus got a Citation to fly just north of the border and get the ID. It was a vehicle being loaded, and when the guys came across Customs picked them up.

"In another case, we had another primary coming up who turned slightly north to Nogales, which is not that unusual, but it caught the attention of the controller who was working it. Why didn't he fly straight? Remember, we get a lot of Mexican traffic who never turn on their transponders, so his being a primary, again, was not unusual. But, in watching this target's specific track, suspiciously looking like he was going to bypass the port of entry, we launched a Citation. As the guy neared the border, we had our aircraft looking at him. What he did was land on a road, one mile south of the border." Houlihan went on to tell that the smuggler was met by three vehicles. A fourth vehicle joined the scene, somewhat complicating the issue for Customs, and then drove away using evasive techniques to throw off any attempts at being tailed. It obviously was the vehicle with the dope. The Citation pilots and the AIO on the FLIR stayed with him, following him to a small house in a residential area half a mile from the Arizona border.

Within twenty-five minutes, Customs agents on the ground coordinated with the Mexican authorities and got a team together to raid that house. Just prior to the team's arrival at the house, the AIO detected a vehicle leaving the house and heading towards the Nogales border point of entry. They advised the border agents who stopped and searched the vehicle when it came across. Much to their surprise, two Sonora state policemen with an automatic weapon were riding in the vehicle! There was no dope but, because Customs had probable cause, they turned the two corrupt officers over to the Mexican federal agents as primary suspects.

As so often happens in Mexico, by the time the raid team hit the house, the bad guys had been advised by local corrupt Sonoran police officers, and it was empty. The house turned out to be a stash house for weapons but no drugs were found.

It is no secret that the Mexican *Federales* and the Sonoran police do not get along very well. Part of the long-standing rivalry is due to jurisdictional conflicts and turf battles between federal and local authorities, most of whom have historically been corrupted by drug money. In any case, the Mexicans are known to be extremely efficient in "extracting" information, real fast, from suspects taken into custody and Customs sometimes benefits from the information, no matter what the source or the technique.

Aerostats

Airborne smugglers still insist on flying across the border to avoid paying middlemen and potential hassles in Mexico. But, since the Aerostats came on line, "it's not easy to come across undetected," Houlihan declares. "If I run the system at a forty-knot filter, which means that anything below forty knots will not show up, the Aerostat will show me *everything* that is moving in a given area above forty knots." He demonstrated that capability by punching some of his magic buttons. Within twelve seconds, the scope became an angry mass of symbology. Pound signs, clutter, ground targets and every airborne target, with its appropriate colored data block, appear within the area that Houlihan has designated, an area whose limits reach far south, into northern Mexico. He punches a few more buttons and turns the Aerostat off, blocking its radar bowl. Within another twelve seconds, seventy-five to eighty percent of the targets fade off the screen.

Surveillance of these known smugglers was under way at Phoenix International when, unbeknownst to all concerned, a Customs P-3 AEW landed. Tucson Air Branch

73

The Orion caused the suspect pilot some concern, and he returned to the terminal. Satisfied that all was well, he took off as planned for Mexico. Tracked by the Aerostat, he picked up a load of dope, flew back to Arizona and air-dropped to a waiting ground crew in the desert. Tucson Air Branch

Which would lead one to question C3I capabilities when the Aerostats are down for maintenance or worse yet, inoperative. "That's when the P-3 AEW comes in," Houlihan claims. "Launch that puppy and we have full radar capabilities once again." Joint Surveillance Sites (JSS) and normal antennas automatically take over when an Aerostat is down. Augmented with Customs sensor birds, NORAD LOWAT radars, P-3s, AWACS, and so on. C3I maintains a twenty-four-hour vigil over American skies. "Although," Houlihan admits, "there are still some clever ways to get around radar, which we won't discuss for obvious reasons." He changes the subject, "Anything you want to see in particular?" Being the curious, intrepid sort, familiar with parts of northern Mexico and the coastlines of the Sea of Cortez, the reply was, "Sure! How about Rocky Point?" He plays his console keys like Liberace, and presto—Rocky Point in all its Spring Break glory! All the way down to Hermosillo, Mexico.

As symbols emerge all over the scope, one stands out: a bright, three-bar, flashing orange block designating a "tagged" aircraft or a hidden law enforcement transponder. It was south of Caborca, slowly moving up from the bottom of the screen. "He's coming north," Jeff muses, and on that note, all visitors were escorted out of C3I.

Aerostats are lighter-than-air surveillance platforms that provide Customs with a reliable, cost-effective radar and communication system for detection of low-flying aircraft. The helium-filled balloons are tethered 10,000 to 15,000 feet above sea level and capable of remaining on station for up to thirty days. Aerostats are unmanned. They are 230 feet long, weigh about 5,000 pounds and resemble the barrage balloons seen over England in World War II. The huge, blimp-like form has an inverted *Y* tail fin on the aft section of the hull, with two lower tail fins spaced at ninety degrees, which stabilize it, facing into the wind. Its skin is made of special material five times stronger than steel. Placed in restricted airspace, out of the way of normal aircraft traffic, there has not been a single aircraft-aerostat accident.

Manufactured by Westinghouse and General Electric, the Aerostat radar system, when fully funded, will cover strategic sections along the entire southern borders of the United States and portions of the Caribbean. The inverted bowls of surveillance are roughly 150 miles in a 360-degree radius. The first Aerostat to go on line, "Cariball I," in the Bahamas, became operational in 1985. The final deployment, slated for completion in 1992, will eventually make up a low-risk, low-cost, low-altitude surveillance fence from the Bahamas to California.

Aerostats provide the only real radar coverage linked to C3I into Mexican airspace. There are six of them across the border; two in Arizona at Yuma and Fort Huachuca, one in New Mexico at Deming, and three in Texas at Marfa, Eagle Pass and Rio Grande City. Because of the state's size, Customs interdiction efforts in Texas would be much more difficult without Aerostat coverage. When the controller at C3I West pulls the menu blocks off of all the targets on a screen over Texas, the Aerostat coverage is clearly identified as awesome! Corpus Christi, Eagle Pass, Brownsville, Laredo—the whole border area becomes almost solid with aircraft and navaid symbols!

In Arizona, there used to be a time when Customs would get three and four sighting reports per night in high-activity smuggling areas like Mohawk Valley. Now, because of the Aerostats, it's pretty quiet. There are days and days on end when Tucson Customs aircrews fly and practice intercepts on each other just to stay proficient. A lot of the dope is simply being trucked up through Mexico or shipped in ocean containers to major US ports.

The First Aerostat Bust in the West

The very first Aerostat bust in the Southwest was back on May 3, 1988. The sequence of events, as related by Scott Eshelman, a supervisor at the Tucson Air Branch, went something like this:

Based upon previous intel and prior smuggling activity involving a Piper Navajo, Customs had had a court-authorized tracking device on this aircraft for about four months. The plane was known to have flown at least one previous low-altitude drug run, using the mountains as radar shields before the Aerostat was completely operational.

On May 2, the bad guys got in the airplane and departed Tucson, bound for Phoenix. "Our agents were conducting full surveillance operations with TV cameras, etc.," said Eshelman, "and waiting for them on the ground at Phoenix. They watched them get out of the airplane, meet two white males, have a short conversation and check into a local motel."

The next morning, the two pilots and one of the white males went back to the airport. "Just as they were arriving," explained Eshelman, "unbeknownst to us, a brand-new Customs P-3 aircraft landed at the airport, for a press conference with Senator DeConcini, and taxied to the ramp near the smugglers' aircraft as these guys were walking out to the Navajo! It must have freaked them out, 'cause they didn't know what was going on."

Remember that this scenario is being photographed. "They hesitated for a moment," Eshelman went on, "and watched the P-3. Then, one of them walked back into the terminal to determine what was going on. When he was told it

The ground crew was forced off the road by this Black Hawk, whose bust crews recovered the dope, arrested the suspects and seized their vehicle. The pickup was outfitted with a CB for communication with the doper pilots. Tucson Air Branch

was a press conference, he walked back to the plane with confidence and proceeded to take off without a flight plan and no transponder."

The Aerostat was operational and once the plane was in the air, Customs personnel at Tucson, via the Aerostat, watched the aircraft's every move. According to Eshelman, the Navajo flew directly to the Mexican border and was eventually lost from C3I radars in Mexican airspace. However, prior intel had it that the smugglers would soon be coming back to the United States.

"That same afternoon, right about shift change [4 P.M.]," said Eshelman, "C3I detected our northbound target flying straight for the Aerostat. In fact, the guys manning the Aerostat on the ground, watched him whiz by at 500 feet AGL," in restricted airspace! By that time the Citation, and a Cessna 210 out of Tucson, had been launched. "The 210 set up for undetected surveillance on the load vehicle on a remote strip on the desert," Eshelman explained, "while the Citation intercepted and tracked him to the area. As soon as the 210 had a visual on the Navajo, the Citation backed off so the smuggler ground crew

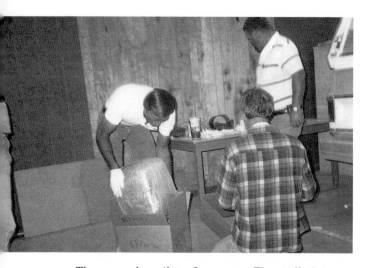

The smuggler pilots flew on to Flagstaff, Arizona, where they were arrested. Despite 1,260 pounds of hard evidence, six felons got off on appeal bond! Tucson Air Branch

would be unaware of their presence. The Navajo landed, off-loaded the dope, 1,260 pounds of marijuana, and within five minutes was airborne, headed northbound again, towards Flagstaff." The Citation followed in close pursuit. Customs alerted all the authorities, launched their King Air out of Davis-Monthan AFB, the Black Hawk out of Phoenix and joined the chase with the Citation.

"Meanwhile," said Eshelman, "the 210 maintained surveillance of the bad guys in the desert, now traveling in a vehicle, and directed a second Hawk into the area to make the apprehension. When the dopers saw the Hawk, they refused to stop on the dirt road. The Black Hawk landed on a dirt trail in front of them, but the truck kept coming so the Hawk pilot took off again." Desperate now, the bad guys pulled off into a wash, bailed out of the truck and tried to escape in different directions on foot. The Black

Hawk landed right behind them, the bust team jumped out, ran through the scrub, caught up with and apprehended two men. They also recovered all the dope.

Back up on the northern scene it was getting dark. The Navajo proceeded to Flagstaff and approached the airport. The Citation broke off the chase and climbed to altitude to direct the operations. "Three minutes before the Navajo lands," Eshelman related, "the King Air lands and waits just off the runway on the taxiway, as do the law enforcement and Customs officers on the airport's perimeter. After the Navajo lands, it taxies to the ramp."

Bear in mind that Customs aircrews do not advertise who they are or what their intentions are in this type of scenario. They make their radio calls just like any pilot would and the Flagstaff Tower hadn't the foggiest idea what was going on. As the Navajo taxied, the King Air moved to block its position, the ground units moved in and the Black Hawk landed directly in front of it using its 30,000 candlepower night sun to illuminate the would-be smugglers. "The bad guys gave up," said Eshelman. "Six individuals were arrested, two in the truck and two in the aircraft. Four sentences were handed out and one pilot is currently in Latuna Prison in Pennsylvania, serving his prison term. The other three are out on appeal bond."

The good news is that, since that time, Customs has indicted and convicted about twenty-five other smugglers associated with that first Aerostat case. Additionally, they have served sixteen search warrants for several safety deposit boxes and five aircraft which are leading to additional arrests and convictions.

Among those corrupted and convicted in this ongoing case were a Philadelphia banker and a US Air Force officer—[an F-16 and A-10 pilot] who was ultimately convicted of transporting 60,000 pounds of marijuana after his identity was discovered.

Part III—Coast Guard Warriors

Chapter 9

The US Coast Guard

A Brief History

US Coast Guard traces its roots in American history back to 1716 when the first lighthouse was built and the Lighthouse Service came into being. In 1789, that service joined the Treasury Department and on August 4, 1790, it was formed into the Revenue Cutter Service. In 1848 the Life Saving Service was formed which eventually merged with the Revenue Cutter Service to form the Coast Guard in 1915. Performing revenue cutter service, life-saving service, steamboat inspection service (under the Department of Commerce) and Bureau of Navigation services for 123 years, the Coast Guard became part of the Department of Transportation (DOT) in 1967.

Headquartered in Washington, D.C., the Coast Guard has two major commands, in New York and San Francisco, with direct operations in the Atlantic and Pacific Oceans. The Coast Guard is at all times an armed force of the United States and equal in status to the Army, Navy, Air Force and Marine Corps, as spelled out in Title 14, United States Code. In peacetime, the Coast Guard serves within the DOT and during wartime, or by Presidential decree, it reports to the Navy Department. Working directly with the Navy and DoD, the Coast Guard is designated as the lead agency for maritime air interdiction.

The Coast Guard protects the nation's right to the living and non-living resources of the seabed, subsoil and waters out to 200 miles offshore. In terms of law enforcement and drug interdiction, they claim their presence "will continue as long as criminals attempt to deliver their poison to our shores."

However, in terms of air interdiction, Coast Guard presence is fairly recent. Back in the late 1970s and early 1980s, when other agencies were beginning to take on serious air interdiction roles, DoD deferred playing (except in face-saving support roles) and argued that a drug interdiction role would hinder performance on national security missions. Capitol Hill, not yet realizing the positive dividends that could be had by the drug war, backed them up. They stated Posse Comitatus restrictions as unacceptable limitations to the armed forces, kept DoD drug interdiction involvement at a minimum and stood their stance until 1989. Posse Comitatus is a federal law which regulates law enforcement action exclusively to law enforcement agencies and personnel.

The Coast Guard, with an ongoing and viable maritime interdiction program, also took exception to a proposed air interdiction role and initially (in 1981) refused offers of dedicated Navy counternarcotic surveillance platforms (E2-Bs and P-3As) to fight airborne smugglers. Their refusal was partly due to maintenance logistics on the aging aircraft and partly due to Coast Guard leadership claims of already having more missions than money. Thus, the Customs Service was named the primary agency for

Pelican choppers make up OPBAT (Operation Bahamas, Turks and Caicos) assets. A Coast Guard crew and their Bahamian counterparts patrol the waters searching for bales of marijuana that reportedly drifted ashore. USCG

the US tactical air interdiction mission against drug smuggling.

As the air smuggler's threat grew to national law enforcement defense proportions in the mid-1980s, Congress began reaping political gain from public antidrug posturing. By then, Customs had acquired an impressive fleet of tactical air interdiction aircraft and had become the envy of rival agencies. To Coast Guard credit, Commandant Paul A. Yost, Jr., sought to re-avow interdiction enforcement authority, a role which Customs contends. In 1986, the Coast Guard entered the narcotics air war as the "lead agency for detection and monitoring for maritime interdiction on the high seas outside a twelve-mile limit." Customs retained its lead in the national air interdiction mission but shares responsibility in the eastern regions (Atlantic Seaboard, Gulf and Caribbean) with the Coast Guard.

Coast Guard Strategy and Aircraft

The Coast Guard divides its air interdiction strategy into three areas: the departure zone (source country), the transit zone (smuggling routes) and the arrival zone (US territories and borders). Out of those three, detection, tracking, and apprehension in the arrival zone is considered the most economically feasible. However, a doper can air-drop, land or off-load anywhere within both the transit and arrival zones, making apprehension a major challenge for the Coast Guard.

Coast Guard provision for maritime air interdiction is determined by early detection, hand-off and apprehension probabilities. These are predicated on detection and interdiction principles based on USAF air defense doctrine which calls for fixed and mobile detection and control assets. Within this surveillance scenario, the Coast Guard employs Airborne Early Warning (AEW) command and control (2C) aircraft.

AEW E-2C Aircraft

By 1987, Navy-provided Coast Guard E-2C Hawkeyes were operational in a dedicated anti-drug role. The Grumman-built E-2C AEW Hawkeye can cruise at 30,000 feet above the ocean with a maximum patrol endurance of five hours at 26,000 feet. Designed for Navy carrier operations, the Hawkeyes are smaller and more compact than Air Force AWACS and are stationed at NAS Norfolk, Virginia, and CGAS (Coast Guard Air Station) St. Augustine, Florida. The E-2C is an all-weather reconnaissance plane with a rotating antenna-radar (twenty-four-foot diameter) disc atop its fuselage which makes it possible for the operators to detect and identify surface, airborne and ground targets for 300 miles in any direction. They can also detect, but not sort, targets beyond the 300-mile envelope. In 1990 the Coast Guard was funded for four counternarcotics-dedicated Hawkeyes, which are now operational. The information provided by the E-2Cs, relayed directly to other aircraft, surface vessels and land-based centers, is a vital component of the surveillance force against drug traffickers in the Southeast.

Within this spectrum, surface, airborne and land targets are detected and tracked by the Hawkeyes whose data, via high resolution, digital, radio-link technology, enable C3I controllers to follow everything the E-2C sees. The tracks of normal commercial, military and civilian aircraft, displayed on 50-, 100-, 200- or 300-mile scopes, are distinguished from the bogeys: unidentified airborne targets that require positive identification if they meet suspect drug profiles. Accurately finding and identifying airborne dopers is much more difficult than detecting military aircraft with IFF (identification friend or foe) devices. To properly respond to a suspected drug flight means a controller notes the codes and alphanumeric designations given all aircraft on the scope, singles out the suspect aircraft, monitors the track, assesses its intentions, makes a decision and recommends a response without ever being absolutely sure the aircraft is a "druggie." If he or she determines the appropriate response requires interceptors, the controller will vector them in for the ID, hand off the target and continue to assist the effort as required.

C-130 Hercules

Another AEW aircraft, the Lockheed C-130 Hercules, is undergoing extensive modifications to meet a similar mission to that of the Hawkeye. The manufacturer has begun development of the new C-130 which is retrofitted with a radome and an APS-125 radar system with display consoles to give it extended long-range sur-

Aerostats can also be surface-based off Navy and Coast Guard ships. Fiber-optics cables feed raw radar information, detected by AN/APS 143(V)2 and AN/APS 128J radars in the balloon, to the ground and C3I. Operational altitudes are zero to 2,500 feet. USCG

veillance capabilities. Its patrol performance is twelve hours on a maximum mission radius of 2,000 nautical miles. Thirty-one C-130s have been assigned to the Coast Guard although only one has been configured to date for the long-range surveillance mission, which would allow the Coast Guard to match the ten-hour endurance levels of P-3 Customs aircraft.

The completion of the DoD MILSTAR (satellite) phase III upgrade for C3I, coupled with GWEN (Ground Wave Emergency Network) and proposed OTH-B sites (which are on indefinite "hold"), would expand the AEW envelopes and make the system the only one in the world. The spectrum of finely tuned networks of permanent, mobile and aerial C3I electronic US platforms would make detection of airborne drug smugglers accessible to all AEW controllers at the punch of a button, no matter where they are. All Hawkeye targets would be automatically detected and tracked. In fact, its crews would be able to track over 600 targets, over water, on land or in the air, while simultaneously controlling over thirty airborne intercepts plus handing off suspected traffickers to Customs and Coast Guard interceptors.

Air Ops East

C3I East in Miami is housed within the confines of the Coast Guard Communications Station in Richmond Heights. Prior to its opening in May 1988, all counternarcotics operations were handled out of the secure Blue Lightning center at Miami FAA Center. Unique to the Coast Guard and a continued point of contention with Customs, C3I East, unlike C3I West, is under joint command by both services as agreed to a few years ago by the Customs commissioner and the USCG commandant. Initially, in July 1988, Customs assumed directorship for a year followed by a year of Coast Guard directorship. In June 1991, the directorship again reverted to Customs with the command rotating every two years thereafter.

Equal to their Customs counterparts, fifteen Coast Guard officers and thirty-two enlisted personnel are presently assigned to the C3I East air interdiction mission.

CGAS Miami

Located at Opa Locka Airport in North Miami, CGAS Miami employs an impressive fleet of rotary and fixed-wing aircraft which make the unit the Coast Guard's largest and busiest air station in the country.

The aircrews fly eleven Falcon HU-25 Guardian jets, four of which are dedicated to the drug interception mission. Two of those are alert birds, always on line and ready, twenty-four hours a day, for fifteen-minute launch. Built by Dassault-Breguet and housing two Garrett ATF 3-6-2C turbofans, the jets were purchased from the Falcon Jet Company to meet Coast Guard requirements for medium-range surveillance. The intercept Falcons have been modified (designated from HU-25A to HU-25C) with similar equipment as the Customs interceptors: AN/APG-66 Fire Control (F-16) radars, WF-360 FLIRs (Customs uses TI FLIRs), and ANVIS-6

Air Ops East display shows south Florida and Bahamian traffic. Every piece of symbology offers vital information for sorting legitimate traffic from illegitimate aircraft. C3I East is under joint command by both Customs and Coast Guard. The controllers must be aware of smugglers' tactics to accurately recommend an intercept. USCG

NVGs (night vision goggles). The Falcon's cruise performance is 410 knots at 40,000 feet with a maximum patrol endurance of 4.5 hours in an 800 nautical mile radius.

Air interdiction operations for initial lead response on targets in the East call for Coast Guard aircrews to rotate alert and launch responsibilities with Customs aircrews. However, both agencies will most often launch assets to back each other up. Additionally, Coast Guard operations require a Falcon be airborne during all E-2C surveillance flights. If necessary, additional Falcons can be launched or diverted from other Coast Guard operations to respond to, or

assist an anti-drug effort. In any case, all information pertinent to the mission is fed into the operations area at Opa Locka where the duty officer is securely linked to C3I, Customs, the tower, the Coast Guard Operations Center, the Rescue Coordination Center and the Surface Law Enforcement Center.

"Miami's AOR [area of operation] is extensive and 'trolling' for dopers can be extensive," says Lt. Comdr. Steve Blankenship who was the pilot on a midnight shift in 1990. "The E-3s and E-2s pick up traffic, along with radar sites in various locations, and planes will be launched out of Gitmo, Puerto Rico or Miami," depending

Designed for Navy carrier operations, the Grumman-built E-2C Hawkeyes can cruise at 30,000 feet above the ocean. Airborne surveillance and intelligence data can be securely relayed to Coast Guard, Customs or ANG interceptors, surface vessels and land-based centers. The E-2C will typically fly four-to-five hour, back-to-back missions for three to four days before its *whereabouts become predictable to air smugglers. Then, the AEW aircraft is forced to move to other areas of operation. Hawkeyes are the Coast Guard's most complex aircraft to fly. The counternarcotics-dedicated Hawkeyes fly over 1,000 hours a year per aircraft. USCG*

on where the suspect is tracked. "The Falcons use a lot of gas when they stay low and slow behind the druggies, which limits their range," he explains. "Other Falcons are often launched to pick up the chase."

Lt. Comdr. Mike Edwards was his copilot, and they explained that when the Coast Guard launches a primary interceptor, normally, a Customs Citation will also remain in loose trail. If the bad guys are tracked to an air drop, the Coast Guard pilots, also known as "Coasties," will remain over the drop scene while Customs follows the smuggler aircraft to landing or back south. "If we can follow the guy all the way back to Colombia, either in the jet or with an E-3," says Blankenship, "we turn the intercept over to Colombian authorities and they will seize the aircraft. Sometimes, when the dopers suspect they are being followed or monitored, they will not off-load. They'll choose to take their chances on evading detection and attempt to return to the source country. In that case, JTF-4 [Joint Task Force-4] will be the folks who know whether or not the guy made it back in country. And, that disposition information is classified," meaning they don't always know if their air interdiction efforts were successful. "If Customs or ourselves are there [when the guy lands]," explains Edwards, "we know what the results are."

Keeping up with trafficking tactics is an unpredictable business. "Oftentimes, we would pick them going up the Gulf," Edwards continues. "Now, they are moving further inland into Mexico. Other routes are into the Bahamas, lower Antilles or right over the top of Cuba. In those cases they drop in the Florida Keys area and go back to Cuban airspace."

"One night," says Blankenship, "prior intel had a target coming north out of somewhere down south, and we had a proposed takeoff time of 2130. We walked out to the jet, got it cranked up and went for it. The guy was cruising VFR at about 1,200 to 1,700 msl and would probably drop down to 500 and come across for the drop.

Hawkeyes must be accompanied by C-130 cargo transports for maintenance and logistic support. USCG

The Coast Guard's Miami Air Station is the largest in the country. Maintenance crews work twenty-four hours a day to keep the fleet operational for rescue and law enforcement missions. Pictured are two Falcon jets and an HH-65A Dolphin helicopter.

We planned on dropping behind him at eleven to twelve point five [intel had figured that his track would lead him alongside Cuba]. We were losing him but the balloon was up and C3I gave us vectors to reacquire him. Now, we have to assume that the guy didn't know whether the surveillance assets at GITMO [Guantanamo Air Base in Cuba] were up, but we know he knows the radar sites and coverage so, we know he's going to avoid those areas and come in low. As it turned out, the guy ended up lost and thanks to no OTH-B, we lost him." Not that it made any real difference that particular night, because chances were, the smuggler landed on a Cuban airstrip.

"Many times," Blankenship comments candidly, "we put covers in those areas and wait to see if they make the run back out of Cuba. You never know when they are going to run and sometimes we get the boats—phenomenal cigarette boats—and sometimes not. We'll park our surface boats right off the ADIZ but, at times, when there is a drop, they'll have a Cuban gunboat in the area just to make sure our cutters don't follow them inside Cuban territorial waters. Typically though, we have stayed away from Cuban vessels."

"JTF is restricted by Posse Comitatus," Blankenship explains, "and disallowed from taking any law enforcement action themselves, so they are a type of watchdog for detection and monitoring. If the Coast Guard has a national vessel, Venezuelan, Panamanian, etc., in international waters and we want to board it, but the master refuses to allow us to board, we have to call back to District [not JTF-4]. They call our Embassy in country who calls that government and says, 'We would like to board this vessel for this reason.' It's called a Statement of no Objection [SONO] and if we have probable cause, once we get the statement, we can board the vessel."

Coast Guard cutters carry Bahamian Navy officers or "shipriders" whose presence permits boarding and seizure authority inside Bahamian waters. For the same reason, the Navy has Coast Guard LEDETS (law enforcement detachments) aboard their vessels who take charge when law enforcement action is required.

"When we get a Statement of no Objection," Mike continued, "we have every right to board the vessel and have jurisdiction at that point. Any vessel destined for a US port, regardless of who, why, what or where, will be registered with US Customs and Coast Guard has the authority to board."

Night Intercepts

When all goes well, a Coast Guard intercept will lead to significant drug seizures and arrests. The following excerpt is taken from aircrew conversations in the Falcon over the night-darkened Caribbean. For uniformity's sake, it merges two actual missions and describes them as one.

A Falcon was vectored to Puerto Rico to intercept a suspected smuggler. The Sensor Operator (SO) acquired the low-level target and the Pilot in Command (PIC) and copilot (SIC, second in command) took a Judy, keeping the Falcon out of sight just above a descending bogey. Their airspeed indicated 124 knots, altitude was 400 feet msl. The SO, in the rear portion of the cabin, was in automatic radar mode. He kept the radar and FLIR locked onto the bogey and relayed the information to the cockpit.

SO: "He's flying low. Watch out." He changed his FLIR picture to black-hot as opposed to white-hot.

PIC: "OK."

SO: "He made a left turn, and a right turn. Yeah, he's making a right turn. He's right rudder flying."

PIC: "OK, keep him out of my altitude. OK Bob?"

SO: "He's at one hundred feet."

PIC: "Roger."

SIC: "He's below us, west of the nose."

PIC: "Gotcha."

The SO switched his radar mode to Autotrack. "Minus ten, twenty-five hundred feet. He's thirty left."

PIC: "OK."

SO: "Twenty-six hundred feet, minus ten."

PIC: "OK."

SO: "Still below one hundred feet."

PIC: "OK."

SO: "Somebody taught this guy his business. Twenty-seven hundred feet, twelve o'clock, eight knots closure. Still below one hundred feet. I'm showing him about five degrees left right now."

PIC: "OK."

SO: "Twenty-five hundred feet separation, four knots of closure. He's feet dry, twenty-five hundred feet negative closure, below one hundred feet."

PIC: "OK."

SIC: "Looks like he's in a right turn."

SO: "You got that."

The pilot followed him and the airspeed indicator nudged 115 knots as the Falcon hung on the edge of a stall. Both the stall and gear warnings blared in the cockpit and the copilot turned them off. If the angle of bank is over fifteen degrees in a low-speed, flaps-and-slats configuration with over 4,000 pounds of fuel, the Falcon will begin to stall. At 200 feet above the ocean, any buffeting is not a pleasant sensation. The pilot glanced at his AOA (angle of attack) indicator, coaxed the throttles slightly forward and swung the Falcon back straight and level.

SIC: "Wait 'till he starts coming."

SO: "Feet wet . . . I got a boat! Go-fast in the water!"

SIC: "Thirty left."

PIC: "OK, coming right." He checked the AOA.

The SO changed to manual track. "Three thousand feet in front of us, thirteen knots closure. He's right on the nose."

PIC: "Contact."

SIC: "He's coming down."

SO: "That last time we were coming across him—a drop! Drop, drop drop!" He punches a button and a tone tells him the computer will automatically record the coordinates of the drop.

When directed, the FLIR screen pans to whatever target the fire control intercept radar is looking at or locked on to. The sensor operator then adjusts the FLIR screen to his liking—black-hot or white-hot. This screen (in black-hot) depicts the suspect target "feet wet" (over water) approaching land. The radar is in air-to-air auto-track. Target information is displayed on the right; fifteen knots negative closure; 500 feet altitude; airspeed 137 knots; heading 135 degrees; two degrees right of the nose; 3,872 feet away. Shown on the bottom left-hand corner is the Falcon's location, airspeed at 136 knots, showing 1,300 foot altitude. Alongside the left side of the screen is L-strobe (radar elevation) which tells how far out the radar is looking. In this case the range is zero to ten miles. At top left is the target's location.

SIC: "I got it!"

PIC: "OK, let's keep with him."

SO: "The drop was over land."

PIC: "Rog."

SO: "Still dropping! Still dropping!" He again tells the computer to record the coordinates. The stall warning in the cockpit goes off and the copilot turns it off.

SO: "I don't see any photo [glow stick] bags—and he's climbing! He's climbing out!

PIC: "OK."

SO: "Eight hundred feet and climbing. The target is at twenty-five degrees right, sir."

PIC: "OK."

SO: "At point eight. Angels point eight. Twenty-eight hundred feet separation, negative closure, flying over the airstrip."

PIC: "You say he's coming left? Is that right?"

SO: "Feet wet, feet wet."

SIC: "He's at six hundred feet."

SO: "He's coming hard left."

PIC: "Keep calling his altitude."

SO: "Angels five hundred, five hundred feet. Twenty-four hundred feet separation, twenty-two knots closure. He's at angels point four."

PIC: "'K."

Suddenly, the target banked left. The radar broke lock and went into boresight, which means the SO had to manually track the target with the FLIR. He calls out, "Lost radar, lost radar. Ahh, holding forty degrees left, fifty degrees lef . . . . "

SIC: "Hard left! Hard left! He's sixty now."

PIC: "OK." He checked his airspeed and the AOA.

SO: "I'll speed up to keep that FLIR. There's uhh, I might be able to get 'im on radar now."

SIC: "OK, sixty."

SO: "I've got 'im fifty degrees left, fifty degrees left. Radar's got 'im."

PIC: "Thanks, coming left thirty."

SO: "OK, he's two thousand feet in front of us."

PIC: "Roger."

The SO got the radar to come back up on computer track, "And he's hard right, he's hard right! Yup! Coming hard 'round again! Target's eighty degrees right . . . seventy degrees right . . . target's sixty degrees right. Got radar back, forty-seven hundred feet separation negative closure, angles one point zero."

PIC: "OK."

SO: "Target's fifty . . . oops . . . I'm going to have to keep it manual." Even though he had automatic tracking capabilities on the radar, he still had to slew the FLIR lens by hand.

PIC: "Yeah. He's sixty right."

SO: "Target's one mile out negative closure."

PIC: "Rog."

SO: "Target's one mile out, fourteen knots closure, angles one point zero."

PIC: "OK, go ahead and put that position in the R-NAV—where the drop is. We're breaking right."

SO: "Say again?"

PIC: "He's landing. We're breaking right."

SO: "Understood."

PIC: "Is he out there?"

SIC: "Yeah."

PIC: "OK."

SIC: "Is our playmate gonna follow him in?"

PIC: "That's a roger."

SO: "There's an airport, and I think it's right there." He slewed the FLIR to the airfield where the twin had just landed. "I got 'im on FLIR, and I got people running! They're running into the bushes! There's people running into the bushes."

PIC: "Coming left, coming right to left."

SO: "There they are. Right there on the FLIR," he said as he boresighted the radar.

PIC: "I see 'em, see 'em FLIRed up."

SO: "OK, when you tip that wing hard, I'm gonna lose them."

PIC: "How 'bout if I turn to the left?"

SO: "Not too hard, this is good right here, I still got 'em. Looks like they're trying to hide now. They're hiding."

PIC: "Can you mark that position?"

SO: "Yeah, it's twenty-five twenty-two north and—I just lost it."

PIC: "OK, I'll speed up your mark. Kevin?"

SIC: "Let's sit tight over it, we should be right down there [he pointed to the FLIR]. I think."

SO: "OK, I got 'em. They're right on the shoreline. There they are! They're hiding in the grass right there! See that lake off to the right, I mean left?"

PIC: "Yeah."

SO: "The helo is right over them—right now! He's got 'em! Right near the edge of the trees. They're just forward of that one tree, the

US Coast Guard seizures for fiscal year 1990 were 30,172 pounds of marijuana and 106,083 pounds of cocaine! USCG

guy's getting ready to walk . . . right on them . . . right in the grass in front of them!"

SIC: "OK, he's right in front."

SO: "He's getting ready to get up off the ground right there! They've got him!"

SIC: "Yeah, they've got 'im."

SO: "They've got 'em both! All right!"

PIC: "OK, they've got them."

SO: "Yaa Hoo!"

BH: "OK, we've got two of the subjects right now."

PIC: "Great!"

SIC: "Looks like there's two more."

SO: "Those are our guys. They're directing a Strike Force in!"

Nine minutes and thirty seconds had elapsed since the SO had called, "He's flying low. Watch out." Within nine minutes more, 1,700 pounds of cocaine, one vessel and one Cessna 404 had been seized, with four suspects (two pilots and two boatmen) arrested.

When a Coast Guard SO or Customs AIO places the cursor on a target and selects auto track, the screen gives him or her all the information needed for an intercept: target latitude and longitude, altitude, course, speed, closure rate and aspect angle. In an intercept, the aspect angle indicates the Falcon's position relative to the target's six o'clock. The FLIR system uses VHS and VLS (very high speed, very large scale) integrated circuitry and two-megabyte memory chips. Its sensor is mounted below the fuselage in a slip ring to allow a 360-degree scan, look-down aspect. The system is integrated with the radar which allows it to automatically lock on to a target via radar cues. The FLIR can also "point" the radar to speed up target reacquisition if the operator loses contact on evasive maneuvers, as was the case during the intercept described. Additionally, secure FLIR and radar imagery and aircraft communications are recorded on a VHS format cassette recorder and are used in debriefs and as evidence in court.

Bottom Line

The US Coast Guard contraband seizures in calendar year 1990 were 106,083 pounds of marijuana and 30,172 pounds of cocaine.

US Coast Guard arrests were 477 and estimated street value of total contraband (including other drugs) was $1,294.5 million.

The majority of the numbers reflected above were seized in 7th Coast Guard District, Miami.

Part IV—Military Drug Warriors

Chapter 10

Department of Defense

The 1989 National Defense Authorization Act required three new roles from the DoD (Department of Defense). First, to be the single lead agency of the US government for the detection and monitoring of aerial and maritime transit of illegal drugs into the United States. Second, to integrate C3I assets into an effective communications network. And third, to enhance the National Guard role to support state drug interdiction and law enforcement operations.

In his inaugural speech, President Bush defined the 1989 DoD act as extremely significant within the counternarcotics arena and stated, "The most immediate threat to securities and the nation is cocaine. There are other drugs out there, but cocaine is the most pervasive and the one that is creating the most problems on our streets right now. It's our number one concern." On September 18, 1989, Secretary of Defense Dick Cheney publicly affirmed the new role as "crucial" in defending the United States from the scourge of illegal drugs. He stated DoD "will employ the resources at its command to accomplish that mission effectively," by designating the detection and countering of the production, trafficking and use of illegal drugs as "a high priority national security mission of the Department of Defense." The 1989 guidance established a strategy for attacking the flow of drugs at the source and transshipment points.

Gen. Colin Powell, Chairman, Joint Chiefs of Staff, was given the responsibility for defining the organizational responsibilities and developing the necessary plans to implement the mission. He, in turn, directed the five CINCs to be responsible for DoD's counternarcotics operations within their AORs (areas of responsibility). The Assistant Secretary of Defense for Reserve Affairs, Stephen M. Duncan, serves as the principal assistant and advisor for all policies and programs of the DoD. The DoD mission calls for the CINCs to gather and process multi-source tactical intelligence information from limited fixed and mobile tactical surveillance assets to assist in apprehending drug smugglers.

CINCNORAD's role is to include the detection and monitoring responsibilities of the DoD. Lt. Col. Tom Hughes states, "DoD's involvement in the war on drugs is a departure from what they normally do . . . the 1989 Defense Appropriations Act washed them into it." Therefore, "along with our air sovereignty mission, we watch over North American airspace looking for drug smugglers." Although, unlike other threats whom "we can shoot down if warranted," he adds, "we can't shoot down drug traffickers because Posse Comitatus restricts DoD from conducting any law enforcement action so CINCNORAD is a major contributor for American and Canadian command and control networks within those countries' counternarcotics program.

"Most of the coca cultivation is in Peru," Hughes explains, "but the transshipment areas for cocaine are Colombia [primarily] and Venezuela. Methodology of transportation is air, airdrop to boats or move it by land. The long-haul aerial methods are aircraft such as corporate jets, O-2s and Turbo Commanders. Some of them are outfitted with modified fuel tanks. Smaller single-engined planes are used for short hops between Latin American countries.

"DoD operates on a chain of command from the SECDEF (Secretary of Defense) to the Joint Chiefs of Staff to the five support CINCs. Given the first, second and third line of defense, DoD is primarily involved in the first line of defense. They share the second line of defense with Customs and law enforcement agencies who also have the third line of defense. But primarily, NORAD works with all the CINCs and Customs for drug interdiction."

CINCFOR coordinates all DoD operational support to counternarcotic activities on the ground, particularly along the southwest border. They provide intelligence analysis, transporta-

The F-16 Fighting Falcon is the world's most sought-after fighter aircraft. When the 1989 National Defense Authorization Act went into effect, it washed America's front-line fighters into the war on drugs. General Dynamics

tion of law enforcement agents, detection and monitoring, use of ground sensors, photo reconnaissance and engineering support activities.

CINCLANT detects and monitors the flow of drugs in international waters and airspace prior to drugs entering US territory. Their airborne drug hunters are E-3 AWACS, E-2 Hawkeyes, P-3 Orions, Seahawks, Sea Sprites, Broncos, Vikings, F-4 Phantoms, F-14 Tomcats and F-18 Hornets.

CINCPAC makes use of the same aircraft, but much of their effort is dedicated to intelligence cueing and data collection for the sorting of drug trafficking vessels. Additionally, they focus on marijuana eradication in Hawaii.

CINCSOUTH also has a strong aerial force, but emphasizes the support and development of host country capabilities by providing training and operational support, material, advice, and technological and maintenance support to the counternarcotics organizations of cooperating nations.

In 1990, DoD counternarcotic flying hours increased 100 percent over 1989 for a total of 40,000 hours! Additionally, a secure DoD communications network known as ADNET (Antidrug Network), comprised of seventy-five sites, allows federal law enforcement agencies to talk with and send data to each other. Eventually, the system will link agents in the field using laptop computers via secure cellular telephones.

To cover the cost of all the above, the DoD counternarcotics budget, which was $439 million in 1989, jumped to $880 million in 1990. The budget for 1991, submitted by the president, sought a total of $1.2 billion which includes

An F-15 interceptor from the 138th Squadron at McChord AFB in Washington patrols the skies at low altitude. The Hughes APG-63 radar used in the F-15 *Eagle is the same as that in the Customs surveillance P-3A Orions.* McDonnell Douglas Corp.

funding for National Guard operations, C3I, law enforcement VHF, UHF, HF communications, satellite communications equipment, interdiction and land border operations, Civil Air Patrol counternarcotics operations, CINC-enhanced counternarcotics initiatives, additional surveillance equipment and procurement of a sector for the OTH-B. However, the budgetary considerations for the OTH-B were shelved in April 1991.

Joint Task Forces

To assist in implementing the Defense Authorization Act, the JTFs were formed in strategic areas across American borders at Alameda, California, El Paso, Texas, and Key West, Florida. All are dedicated to the antidrug detection and monitoring missions.

The missions of the JTFs are (1) to detect and monitor suspect aircraft and surface operations; (2) to integrate C3I networks; (3) to coordinate detection and monitoring activities of other federal agencies; (4) to provide DoD intelligence to law enforcement agencies; and (5) to assist in coordination of DoD and civil agency resources to eliminate duplication of effort.

Although the JTFs have no direct intercept and apprehension mission, their efforts are beginning to seriously impede the smuggling trade. Regardless of the fact that not all players are reading off the same sheet of music, and regardless of disagreements on how to conduct JTF operations, the impasse generated by these nag-

In support of the DoD antidrug efforts, ANG units around the country and in Puerto Rico assist in aerial *and maritime detection and monitoring of aircraft and vessels suspected in smuggling activities.*

ging difficulties is overshadowed by DoD's commitment to the threat.

Both the East and the West are areas of JTF operations classified as target-rich environments. Sorting legitimate targets from illegitimate targets within JTF AORs is extremely difficult due to the tremendous volume of air and sea traffic. It begins as close to the source as possible and requires a focused intelligence effort, the key to effective operations.

There are two types of intelligence: threat assessment intelligence and real-time intelligence. Threat assessment intel is classified as early detection and monitoring to allow law enforcement prepositioning for interception. Action is based on generic patterns of intelligence which are updated as operations change in response to smugglers' tactics. Real-time intelligence is specific to immediate deployment of assets.

JTF's first priority is to respond to real-time intelligence, and that's where critical coordination between the JTFs and law enforcement agencies comes in. Via a system called JVIDS (Joint Visual Integrated Display System) day-to-day coordination with law enforcement becomes possible. JVIDS is a dedicated computer system which shares intelligence and presents a graphic representation of ongoing counternarcotic operations, allowing (near real-time) communications between Customs, Coast Guard, DEA, FBI and JTF.

The DoD is the lead agency for detection and monitoring of aerial and maritime transit of illegal drugs into the United States. Two ANG F-16 Falcons patrol the coast of Florida.

Air War Won?

On May 29, 1990, morning headlines across the nation proclaimed "Air War On Drugs Won!"

Three Congressmen, members of the House Armed Services Investigations Subcommittee, just back from five southwest border sites— EPIC (DEA's El Paso Intelligence Center), JTF 6 in El Paso, Texas, the San Isidro Customs Port of Entry, Air Ops West (C3I) at March AFB in California, and JTF 5 at Moffett AFB in California—declared, "The air battle has for all practical purposes already been won." The three gentlemen were Nicholas Mavroules (D-Massachusetts), Chairman, Investigations Subcommittee, Lane Evans (D-Illinois) and Jim McCrery (R-Louisiana).

Most people associated with air interdiction do not agree with that statement, believing, instead, that the airborne smuggler remains a threat. He is cunning, flexible, adaptive, un-

The aging F-4 Phantom II is mostly employed in the war on drugs as a reconnaissance platform. However, the few units that have not yet converted to modern fighter aircraft have, for the past two years, participated in other counternarcotics missions.

predictable and loaded with cash. He exploits our air defense weaknesses and border limitations with tenacity. He applies defensive countermeasures that would stagger the lay mind. He understands law enforcement strategies and tactics better than Congress, and he probably got a good laugh out of those headlines!

One would venture to say that the three gentlemen in question have yet to call on an aviation branch, speak to a professional airborne drug hunter or fly in an interceptor!

The morning's article stated "Chairman Les Aspin (D-Wis.) of the full committee," to whom the three reported, "praised the report. 'We are in a war with the drug industry,' Aspin said. 'And, as in any other war, we must stay one step ahead of the enemy or he'll leap a step ahead of us.'"

In their report to the chairman, the members stated that it was important for the American public to understand "we are winning the air war against the drug lords. That should soon be history. The administration's plans are geared to the threat that is going away rather than the threat that is growing our way. We must pledge ourselves to avoid the body-count syndrome. If air interdiction fails totally or succeeds beyond our wildest expectations, the result either way will be a drop in seizures." Chairman Aspin agreed, saying, "This report warns us all against fighting yesterday's battles noting that many people, including myself, have

JTF's priority is to respond, real time, to counternarcotics intelligence data. The F-4s have been known to put the fear of God into a smuggler—in the air and on the surface!

questioned the utility of the air interdiction program."

In fairness to the committee, the Mexican-American land border battle was accurately identified as a current threat, and "a proposal was laid out for closer cooperation with Mexico to catch drugs at their landing sites before they can be broken down and dispersed." Last, but not least, "In the final analysis, education is the true solution to the drug problem." A true statement.

The Mexico Problem

When the success of the air interdiction program in the Southeast forced the airborne drug smuggler to create southwestern routes, both the United States and Mexico were unprepared to deal with the resulting problem. The lack of American foresight in recognizing that the obvious solution for the drug cartel would be to move west evolved into an international political, strategic and tactical nightmare.

The smuggler's preferred landing and off-loading sites in Mexico are his safe haven. The United States respects Mexico's right to territorial sovereignty, does not suggest that they waive those rights, and cannot, will not, touch those criminals without the agreement and assistance of the Mexican government. The answer lies in Mexico's willingness to cooperate with the United States and in the United States' willingness to provide counternarcotic ground and air defense training and assets to Mexico.

Presently, half of the land border, from California to New Mexico, is reasonably protected by Aerostats. Those assets, subject to nature's whims—high winds, thunderstorms, ice storms, and so on—are not always operational. To compound the problem, the land and Gulf borders between Texas and Mississippi have yet to be covered by the Aerostat radar fence and are exploited on a daily basis by dopers.

If Mexico would grant overflight rights for unarmed US sensor birds, it would help tremendously and pose no threat to Mexico. By the same token, America could grant overflight rights to the Mexicans without posing a threat. It is a dichotomy of sorts that smuggler aircraft, loaded with illegal narcotics and weapons, flown by heavily armed pilots who blatantly violate Mexican laws, can make twenty-four-hour use of sovereign airspace and territory barred to legitimate US surveillance and law enforcement aircraft.

Because the drugs are destined for US markets and because the border war is primarily a US war, the United States could make a deal, as they did with Saudi Arabia during the Gulf War. Mexico allows US counternarcotic and surveillance action in and over their country, and the United States reciprocates, plus funds any and all Mexican budgetary concerns involving this type of border action. Mexico gets to keep billions in cash, dope seizures, planes, cars, boats and weapons. The United States gets to reduce the influx of drugs. Mexico benefits from a reduction in lawlessness, the United States gets to reduce drug-related crime.

Mexico's Effort

Mexico's war on drugs is fought on the ground.

The Mexican government claims it combats drug trafficking in order to secure the health of its citizens, its national security and participation in international cooperation. Their war is waged primarily through preventive programs and corrective measures via law enforcement action and rehabilitation programs.

According to the AGR, Attorney General of the Republic, Mexico's national jurisdiction includes investigation and pursuit of drug trafficking and drug-related crimes, both of which constitute federal offenses.

In accordance with Mexican law, the armed forces, to guarantee national security, can carry out civic action connected with trafficking and assist federal authorities in drug eradication. The Army can locate and destroy illicit plantings, dismantle clandestine labs, break up drug networks, but are precluded from arrest procedures unless dopers are caught in the act.

Mexico's permanent campaign against drug trafficking was established in the early 1980s with the help of $10 million a year from the US State Department. The system, since then, has been plagued with corruption and turf wars. The situation caused tremendous grief to resident DEA agents in the field, particularly those in the northwestern states of Mexico where powerful Mexican drug lords were firmly entrenched. The drug magnates had formed a "Guadalajara Cartel" with three men at the helm: Ernesto Fonseca Carrillo, Rafael Caro Quintero and Miguel Angel Felix Gallardo. They shipped tons of heroin, cultivated thousands of desert acres of sinsemilla marijuana, created a direct Colombian-US cocaine pipeline and became the largest traffickers in the Western hemisphere. At one point Felix Gallardo was moving two tons of cocaine a month to US destinations, with much of the contraband being smuggled by air.

Fighting a war with one hand, often two, tied behind their backs, DEA field agents in Mexico lost agent Kiki Camarena to the war on drugs in 1985.

In 1986, both Fonseca Carrillo and Caro Quintero were captured and imprisoned in Mexican federal prisons—where they remain to this day. Two years later in 1988, President Salinas

This well-worn, multi-xeroxed, multi-faxed cartoon of a "U.S. Customs F-4" (which was passed around Customs aviation units from Puerto Rico to California) reflects the true sentiments of many Customs warriors.

de Gortari, intent on wresting power away from corrupt party officials, established an office to the Assistant Attorney General to investigate and combat drug trafficking. In 1989, AGR agents captured the DEA's most wanted man: Felix Gallardo. The office also initiated a two-month special operation in northern Mexico to discourage drug trafficking activities. Employing army, federal, state and municipal manpower and assets, the AGR claims eighty-three strategic check points were established, 180 hectares of illicit crops were eradicated, 105,981 kilos of drugs were seized and 2,582 suspects were arrested.

Finally, in 1990, the office was given authority for the general coordination of all agencies to intensify the war on drugs. Mexican counternarcotic aviation assets include fifty-five Bell 206 spray helicopters, eleven Bell 212 transport helos, twenty-nine Cessna 206 reconnaissance aircraft and fourteen other fixed-wing airplanes. Most of the aircraft were supplied by the United States and are employed in aerial spraying and eradication missions. None are sensor-equipped.

Mex-US Bilateral Issues

In 1987, a Mexican-US treaty was signed covering the prevention, investigation and pursuit of drug trafficking offenses (among other crimes), and providing mutual jurisdictional agreements between the two countries.

In 1988, an agreement outlining joint cooperation on combating drug trafficking and drug dependence, subscribed by both countries, paved the way for specific action to combat drugs.

The agreement is subject to internal laws and stipulates that the parties shall consult each other in regard to intended or proposed actions involving counternarcotic operations.

Nine meetings in five years have been held between the attorneys general of the Mexican border states and the state attorneys for southwestern US states on drug trafficking and other matters. Agenda highlights during these meetings were: mutual legal assistance and extradition fees; strengthening action and procedures to fight drug traffic and firearms smuggling; control and regulation of chemical inducers; money laundering and breaking up criminal organizations.

According to Mexican effort statistics from December 1, 1988, to January 27, 1991, 15,669 hectares of illicit crops were eradicated with 977,627 kilos of marijuana and 83,857 kilos of cocaine seized. Twenty-three thousand six hundred seventy-two suspects were arrested. Air incidents were noted as sixty-nine. No mention was made in the report of any plans for law enforcement overflight rights, either way.

Chapter 11

The Air National Guard

To help fight the war on drugs, the National Guard's Drug Interdiction Support Program, under the command and control of state governors, provides invaluable support to law enforcement agencies. These missions include observation and reporting, air and ground transportation, loan of specialized equipment, commercial cargo inspection, radar surveillance and aerial imagery.

Total allocation of fiscal year 1990 funds for the Guard was split into $60,182,000 for the Army National Guard and $16,192,000 for the Air National Guard (ANG). ANG antidrug missions include ground and air surveillance and reconnaissance, aerial photo reconnaissance and transportation sorties. To support these missions, a $40 million procurement package has been approved for aerial AN/TPS radar and FLIR systems, enhanced communication systems, aircraft search lights, Loran C avionics, portable Lorans and OH-58 aircraft upgrades.

High-dollar, high-value technology is not the Guard's greatest asset, but the availability of their volunteer part-timers who fight the war on drugs. These warriors are part of the total force and part of the counternarcotics war at the same time that most of them manage two separate occupations and a personal life.

For over 200 years, the citizen soldier has answered the call to arms in every US conflict and has always maintained a traditional role in assisting their communities. For many, especially those with families, that role has hit home.

The war has been declared and no state in the union is immune. It takes place in the air, on the ground and on the coasts. In ports from Seattle to San Diego, from New York to Corpus Christi, thousands of containers arrive daily which often conceal drugs. Now, because of National Guard troops, ports like Miami can search 100 percent of those targeted by Customs, whereas, before the Guard pitched in, only 30 to 40 percent were searched. That job entails a full stripping out of the container and conducting a complete examination of the cargo. It is grueling, tedious work done in temperatures from twenty degrees below zero outdoors to 150 degrees inside the container. To effectively search some of the cargo, such as foodstuffs, a special probe is jammed into barrels or sacks to find cocaine.

Operation Guardian

Operation Guardian, as the National Guard operation in support of the war on drugs is called, has led to major discoveries of illegal drugs. On April 28, 1989, more than 2,500 pounds of cocaine were found onboard a Brazilian airliner at Miami International Airport; street value was $103 million! Less than a month later, two other shipments were intercepted before they hit the streets at $15.5 million. "Success," claims the Guard, "is when you don't find it, because you know that the smugglers are looking for other ways to get it in. They don't want to challenge the search capability that National Guard warriors have added to the Customs efforts."

Part of the Guard's mission, in support of state and local law enforcement, is to provide air and ground support in locating and destroying illicit drug crops. One relatively small hidden field of marijuana can yield $250,000 or more. High grade marijuana is worth approximately $1,000 a foot and a mature plant will grow to six feet! It's tough to find the fields and sometimes dangerous to destroy them.

Guard aircraft employed in the war on drugs are C-130s, OV-1s and other fixed-wing and rotor aircraft. Fighter aircraft used by the Guard are front-line F-15 and F-16 interceptors and reconnaissance RF-4s. Additionally, A-7s, OA-10s and OA-37s are employed in observation, photo reconnaissance and support roles.

In fiscal year 1990, the Guard performed over 4,700 counternarcotics missions. As one guardsman put it, "It may be the Guard's most important mission . . . and the most rewarding, because we live in these communities and our kids go to school here. When drugs come into our states, we like to think that everything we stop is one less thing that our kids will be tempted with."

The Interceptor Role

The Air National Guard (ANG) is a formidable deterrent to the airborne drug smuggler.

The air defense role, as played by ANG fighters, is described by the director of combat operations for NORAD, Maj. Gen. Eric Ian Patrick, CF. "CINCNORAD's role within the monitoring/detection mission, insofar as fighters being launched on VID [visual identification] of a smuggler airplane, is strongly tied in with prior intelligence. First, we will look at a timeline. When did he leave? What was his speed, etc.?

If necessary, NORAD can launch interceptors to ID a suspect aircraft. ANG interceptors can maintain visual and radar contact without being seen.

Two alert F-16s, from the 150th Fighter Interceptor Group at Jacksonville and their Detachment 1 at *Homestead AFB, are always ready to launch against any suspected or known hostile intruder.*

Then, we assess that information with ground radars and/or other systems which will allow us to identify him. Third, because we are all in on the same intelligence network, we call Customs, the law enforcement agents, DEA, etc., and ask 'are you doing anything on this contact?'

"Another type of operation is when someone in the field says 'hey, we don't have anybody working this target.' At that point we look at the situation and, if necessary, provide air defense fighter resources on CAP (combat air patrol) or alert. When the E-3 picks up the guy, he will vector the fighters towards the target.

"Occasionally, a fighter pilot will ID an airplane during the day. They are trained to fly a profile where they can maintain radar or visual detection of the target without being seen, via single-ship figure eight patterns, two-ship waves and CAP patterns, where the target is always in radar lock.

"If, on a rare occasion, fighters are needed for a night intercept on a suspected, high profile, inbound target, NORAD will most often put up a B model, a two-seat F-16 or F-15 where the pilot in the back seat flies with NVGs (night vision goggles), only to confirm the type of aircraft, not the numbers.

"For the disbelievers who say, 'Why are you wasting so much fuel on launching fighters that can't do that [low and slow intercept] mission?' we say that it is part of our mission. The guy has violated the ADIZ, he is hostile and attempting to elude authorities with million-dollar loads of illegal contraband. The only time fighters are specifically launched to ID a suspected drug runner is when there is no other option. Then, our pilots are trained to deal with that situation and will act accordingly."

Florida Intercept Warriors

The 125th Fighter Interceptor Group (FIG), commanded by Col. Buddy Titshaw in Florida, became the first ANG unit to operate the F-16s in a dedicated air defense role. Headquartered at the Jacksonville International Airport, the unit's full-time mission is to intercept unidentified aircraft that venture into or purposely violate the American ADIZ. The 125th FIG has a detachment (DET 1) at Homestead AFB which is commanded by Lt. Col. Jack McDougall.

DET 1's location in south Florida, has put it in the heart of operational counternarcotic opportunities; a target-rich environment where practically every pilot in the unit has had the chance to intercept unarmed but tricky adversaries in single- and twin-engined, general aviation aircraft.

"Our job, insofar as drug interdiction, is really our normal job," says McDougall. "When somebody comes across the ADIZ, it doesn't matter if he's a druggie or a military airplane from a different country. We have to know who he is. If the flight path fits the drug profile, and prior intel is available, it's a suspected drug run and Customs or Coast Guard will launch their aircraft and react with those resources. However, we also are available and we can back them up if necessary. Let's say it looks like a Customs profile, but it comes from an area like Cuba where the target could be something else. We're not going to sit back and let a MiG-23 fly in here at 180 knots, simulating a civilian aircraft!"

Sorting traffic is Customs' responsibility, but when they get more traffic than they can effectively handle, or get targets further away than they can respond to, it makes more sense for ANG to make the intercept and identification.

"There are a lot of different ways to detect and sort traffic," continues McDougall, "and through those systems (assuming they are working) we determine the response. If and when a radar site has a planned 'down time,' we will have planned 'up times' with other ground

RF-4C Phantom IIs line the ramp of the 163rd Tactical Reconnaissance Group at March AFB. Photo reconnaissance is one of the most significant missions performed by the ANG in support of counternarcotics operations.

and air surveillance capabilities. We always try to fill the gaps. If it becomes difficult to do that, we will launch. If and when we assist on an intercept—and it takes a lot of effort and concentration to fly an F-16 low and slow—once a successful drug intercept is made, it is always handed over for Customs to make the bust."

DoD CAP missions can get into "questionable use of the resource," says McDougall, "and what I have recommended is the following. Whenever we are deadheading or, if we are launched but the mission is cancelled before we ever get gear in the well, I recommend that we go ahead, take that resource and do a job! If we are short on monitoring, do it! Go out and look! However, that is not one of our requirements. Personally, I believe we could do more with what we've got.

"I've picked up guys, when deadheading from Jax, by looking for targets of opportunity just to report back to the FAA. In one instance, the FAA didn't have a clue as to who the guy was and gave me the authority to coordinate directly with C3I. They alerted Oakgrove GCI who coordinated the intercept and I went in to ID him. When the guy saw the F-16, he turned around and went back to Jamaica. Sometimes they want us to remain undetected but in this case, scaring him off was C3I's objective.

"On another instance, when I was deadheading again, Customs was looking for a guy that I just happened upon. I capped him into Marathon and called the Black Hawk in on him. By the time Customs arrived, he had disappeared behind a hangar and they couldn't distinguish him from other aircraft on the airfield. My field of view, as I capped over the airport, allowed me to watch him. So, I told them, 'It's the yellow airplane behind the second highwing on your left,' and they busted him.

"It pays to look for targets of opportunity. My little book of tricks has everybody that has anything to do with drug interdiction or SAR (search and rescue) listed, with their freqs. If I see Border Patrol or Marine Patrol doing something, I can punch in their frequencies and offer assistance. That information is available to all our pilots. However, if they happen upon a given situation, the extra effort to find out if some assistance is needed or warranted, is up to them."

It does not seem probable that ANG will receive additional drug interdiction tasking. The Congressional proposition to shoot down drug planes failed on a forty-eight to fifty-two vote in 1990. "There's always the question on shootdown authority," McDougall admits thoughtfully. "I suppose that if you really want to get their attention we can blow them out of the sky. However, my thoughts are, since it is not a capital offense to bring drugs into the country, until they decide to make it a capital offense the ANG tasking won't change except perhaps to enhance our equipment, and put up additional assets and surveillance sites."

California Recce Guardians

Photo reconnaissance (recce, pronounced "wrecki" for short) is typically provided by RF-4C units and is one of the most significant missions performed by the ANG in support of drug interdiction. Additional recce and tactical intelligence through surveillance of target areas such as border crossing points, abandoned airstrips, and so on, is provided by Special Forces, long-range reconnaissance patrols, other ANG units and Civil Air Patrol. These missions are usually performed in addition to the regular mission and training activities of the Guard and Civil Air Patrol.

All of these missions focus on areas, not individuals, and garner critical drug operation information which is passed immediately to supported law enforcement agencies.

Lt. Col. Dave Hudlet, commander of the 163rd Tactical Reconnaissance Group (TRG) at March AFB explains the unit's involvement.

"The mission began as the demand for recce support grew, and is one which interfaces with other DoD and law enforcement units. In California, we work with Operation Alliance who are set up to coordinate the military mission for the organization."

Operation Alliance

Operation Alliance, devised by Customs in 1986, is a joint federal, state and DoD command which unites law enforcement agencies, backed by military resources, to fight the entry of illegal drugs along the southwest border. Headquartered at the Tactical Operations Center in Houston, the program has Mexico's blessing and incorporates investigations of major drug-trafficking rings and money-laundering operations along the border. To that end, the FBI, DEA, IRS and ATF (Bureau of Alcohol, Tobacco and Firearms) are some of the players. Within Operation Alliance guidelines, the Coast Guard shares the responsibility for maritime interdiction with Customs, and the DoD role is one of sharing assets while their strategists contribute detection expertise.

In terms of photo reconnaissance, DoD members of the Operation Alliance team determine what can be done by the recce units to combat the drug threat. Once that is established, they send the law enforcement request to the JTF, who send it back to the National Guard at state level, and they call the recce unit to find out if the mission is feasible. "We don't take every request that comes down the pike," adds Hudlet. "Not only because the cost for these missions comes out of a DoD pot designated to the drug program, but because we're *tactical* reconnaissance, not strategic. If you say, 'I need some information from this intersection, one mile down this road, to this intersection,' we can do that. But, if you need big area searches . . . our aircraft would come back with thousands of feet of film. It's unpracticable."

The 196th Tactical Reconnaissance Squadron (TRS), under the 163rd TRG, recently converted from flying F-4E fighters to RF-4C recce Phantoms. The squadron operations officer, Maj. Mike Stanton, says the unit maintains a state and federal mission which calls for providing tactical reconnaissance to all friendly forces. It is a mission accomplished via a system of onboard visual, optical, electronic and other state-of-the-art cameras and sensors.

The RF-4C Phantom II is a long-range, multi-sensor fighter capable of all-weather day and night reconnaissance. The Phantom can fly from 100 to 55,000 feet agl, at speeds in excess of 600 mph. The cameras, sensors, radar and

To retrieve the infrared film for processing, the crews break open the nose of the Phantom where the optical cameras and sensors are located. With optical cameras such as those on the RF-4C, reconnaissance efforts on October 30, 1990 yielded a subterranean drug operation in Mojave, Arizona, which resulted in seizure of 14,547 cultivated marijuana plants. Street value was estimated at $7.3 million. ANG

electronic recce systems are primarily operated by the backseater. The optical equipment is normally used for day, low-altitude ops and can produce forward-looking oblique imagery, vertical and mapping imagery, and horizon-to-horizon panoramic imagery. Additionally, special long-range optical photographic systems, with focal lengths from thirty-two to sixty-six inches, can provide incredibly detailed prints from extended standoff ranges.

The infrared sensors are employed for high-altitude, covert nighttime operations. They locate targets by detecting heat sources and heat differentials. The system records the infrared image on film. Because this process is a continuous one, it can produce a map of the areas under the Phantom's flight path.

The side-looking radar is a day-or-night, all-weather system that records a high-definition radar picture on film, of images on either side of the aircraft's flight path—mountains, canyons, and so on. The tactical electronic reconnaissance system also records on tape the identity and location of electronic emitters. Both systems are data-linked to ground processing sites and intelligence centers.

All the black-and-white imagery processing, including optical and IR systems, is done by the squadron, taking about thirty minutes. "We have onboard color capabilities," Stanton adds, "which is processed elsewhere, on a three-day turnaround."

There are five reconnaissance groups across the country tasked to support the anti-drug mission. Geographic locations determine their level of involvement. Five to seven percent of all sorties for the 196th are narcotics related and the unit expects that to grow as their capabilities and assets grow. "We are hoping to get into the border act," says Stanton. "The way

The ANG and Reserve Test Center in Tucson is the single point of contact for Guard and Reserve fighter aircraft test operations. Among the items the Center has addressed in the last year are the APG-66 radar systems used by F-16 Falcon and Customs Citation interceptor aircrews.

offers. "The pilots don't have an air-to-air radar to work, it is not as 'switchology' intensive and in some respects it's simpler. On the other hand it is demanding because we generally have multiple targets with different parameters for each target. That requires thinking in terms of integrating two airplanes to make the passes and get the photos. Plus, you have to consider the needs of the folks that you are flying the mission for. We need to give them what they want to see on film."

Night Vision Devices

All pilots—Customs, Coast Guard, ANG, USAF, Navy, commercial, corporate, private, even smugglers—do not care for night flying, flying close to the ground or over water at night. "No matter what cosmic systems you give them, they simply prefer to fly during daytime," said Lt. Col. Bob Fosnot, director of operations for the ANG AFRES Test Center (AATC) in Tucson, Arizona. "Night flying is not a skill that comes naturally and most pilots tend to fight it," he explained. "It defies their ability as stick-and-rudder technicians and places them in an abstract element further limited by lack of natural nocturnal senses, night focus and body-rhythms."

Yet, practically every pilot associated with combating or perpetrating the war on drugs uses night vision devices (NVDs). It is an arena where night vision enhancement is essential. An arena in which the AATC has successfully developed and tested the way NVDs are used.

The AATC develops and tests hardware, software and tactics for Guard and Reserve fighter operations. To improve DoD counternarcotic programs, and support law enforcement assets in the field, the AATC addresses those needs at the squadron or user level and shares joint test items and programs with Customs to improve (and trade ideas on) drug interdiction equipment, tactics and strategies. "When an upgrade is needed or an item identified," explained Fosnot, "the test center concentrates on a low-risk, off-the-shelves, state-of-the-art solution so we can field tactics to the units, and software or hardware on the aircraft, quickly.

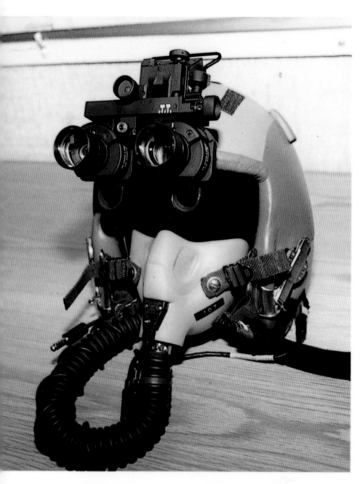

NVGs, also known as HMDs (helmet mounted displays), such as those depicted in this photo, were tested by AATC pilots for counternarcotic night operations. The Cats Eyes NVGs are manufactured by GEC Avionics. AATC

things are going we may be picking up a new sensor that was used in Desert Storm, and its use will expand our national mission as well as our state mission. One of the nice things about flying the RF-4 is now both our national and state missions dovetail together. It's super training.

"Compared to a fighter-bomber mission, the recce mission is reasonably simple to fly," he

"Many of the items that the AATC has recently addressed, apply to fighter counternarcotic operations," Fosnot added. "Of these, the HMDs (helmet mounted displays) and NVDs are of significant importance to night operations in the aerial drug war. Our pilots were among the first to fly NVD operations in the F-16. They helped develop tactics and procedures for use in the cockpit by defining which kind of devices are best suited for anti-drug missions at night." As a result of the AATC's efforts, both Customs and DoD pilots are more confident with night missions; with systems and aircraft equipped with the technology to fly the mission effectively and tactically, with higher percentages of survivability.

A Florida Air National Guard (FANG) decal.

Part V—Civilian Drug Warriors

Chapter 12

Civil Air Patrol

All pilots, international airports, municipal airports, private airfields, fixed base operators (FBOs), flight schools, aero clubs and aviation organizations are adversely affected by air smuggling. Every person associated in any way with general aviation is directly affected. How? Through stolen aircraft, higher insurance premiums, strict new regulations, restrictions on international travel by private and corporate flyers and new and revised aircraft and modification requirements. Every plane that takes off, regardless of intentions, point of departure or destination, is subject to legal monitoring and even interception if they come close to meeting a suspected drug smuggling profile.

One organization and its pilots is doing something about this dilemma by confronting the air smuggling problem head on, and supporting the Customs air interdiction mission from coast to coast, border to border, and then some.

Headquartered at Maxwell AFB in Alabama, Civil Air Patrol (CAP) is the official civilian auxiliary of the US Air Force and is charged by law with the inland search and rescue mission for the continental United States. Older than the Air Force, the Civil Air Patrol was created on December 1, 1941, under the Office of Civil Defense, as an emergency measure to make civilian aviation resources available to the national defense effort.

During World War II, CAP men and women flew thousands of coast patrols looking for enemy submarines. Strapping depth charges, demolition bombs and even clusters of grenades onto makeshift rails of private aircraft, the CAP dawn patrols sank at least two enemy subs. In addition to its maritime role, CAP flew dawn-to-dusk border patrols from Texas to Arizona, on the watch for spies, saboteurs and suspicious activities. CAP's wartime efforts include 86,685 missions (244,600 hours) of coastal patrol; 30,000 flying hours of border patrols; 173 enemy subs sited, eighty-three bombs dropped, sinking 2.5 subs; 363 victims of sub attacks saved; and 4,720 (30,033 hours) land border patrol missions. Ninety CAP aircraft were lost, with sixty-four pilots and observers killed in action, and seven wounded.

Civil Air Patrol went down in the annals of American history as the organization with more downright unselfishness and self-sacrifice invested than any other volunteer group.

Following its wartime service, Civil Air Patrol was chartered by Congress on July 1, 1946, as a volunteer, nonprofit corporation. Two years later, on May 26, 1948, Congress granted Civil Air Patrol status as the civilian auxiliary of the Air Force. Since that time, CAP volunteers have continued a record of solid performance and dedicated public service in three missions,

Emergency Services, Cadet Programs and Aerospace Education.

Today, fifty-two CAP wings (one for each state plus Washington, D.C., and Puerto Rico), with 19,000 radio stations, 6,500 aircraft and over 60,000 members, fall under the command of Brig. Gen. Warren J. Barry, Civil Air Patrol, Maxwell AFB. Wartime and peacetime missions under Emergency Services include search and rescue, civil defense, disaster relief and RADEF (aerial radiological monitoring) sorties. And now, one more national mission has been added to the Civil Air Patrol.

CAP Counternarcotics Mission

On November 14, 1985, Civil Air Patrol, the Air Force and Customs entered into an agreement whereby CAP would assist Customs by performing air surveillance and reconnaissance patrol flights along US borders and coasts in support of the government's drug interdiction effort. Restricted by Posse Comitatus, the CAP counternarcotics program does not involve its aircrews in law enforcement action. The mission was initiated in Florida in 1986, and today qualified CAP aircrews fly about half of the Customs daytime reconnaissance patrol flying hours across the nation.

CAP (Civil Air Patrol) flies thousands of counternarcotics missions every year in support of the national effort in the war on drugs. CAP

Additionally, on April 19, 1989, a similar agreement was entered into with DEA and the US Forest Service (USFS) whereby CAP provides aircraft and qualified aircrews to assist DEA and USFS in aerial reconnaissance for detection of illicit drugs, primarily marijuana, within the United States, its territories and possessions. Once again, CAP members are prohibited from participating in apprehension or detention procedures or search, arrest and seizure action.

According to the agreement, Customs, assisted by Civil Air Patrol commanders, provides special briefings on the mission, its responsibilities, dangers and restrictions. The sessions are given to qualified CAP members pursuant to acceptable background checks, individual SOUs (Statement of Understanding) and Customs clearance on all participants. Once these steps are accomplished, CAP members are cleared to fly the missions subject to wing directives. Command and control of CAP resources remains with CAP wing commanders at all times and flight operations are conducted in accordance with CAP directives.

All CAP counternarcotics (CN) missions are assigned to Customs by the Air Force after being established and coordinated with Customs by the National CAP CN director, Col. Harold W. Bowden, headquarters, NAS Dallas, Texas.

Basically, the CAP counternarcotic mission boils down to being additional eyes and ears for Customs, DEA and the Forest Service. Their CN role is generally restricted to aerial reconnaissance, data gathering, communications support and airlift of law enforcement personnel. However, CAP has also simulated the flight patterns

CAP was begun as a coastal civilian defense effort against German submarine "wolfpacks" that ter- *rorized Allied shipping lines along southeastern US shores. CAP*

of drug smugglers to train ANG, NORAD and federal agency pilots and personnel. The majority of CAP's efforts have been concentrated in the southeastern and western areas of the United States, but due to the increased demand for their services, the missions have now expanded into all areas of the country.

With this in mind, CAP forces can be used in grid searches to locate, map and photograph clandestine airstrips and search for activity in known drug smuggling areas. Additionally, they can fly aerial reconnaissance missions, conduct recce photography operations and routine coastal and border patrols. They can serve as aerial communications platforms for surveillance or detection operations in remote areas and do periodic checks of lake beds used as airstrips.

To this end, the Customs National Aviation Center reported CAP enforcement seizure and arrest results for 1989 and 1990 were beyond their expectations. Thousands of sorties were flown by CAP pilots who logged a total of 21,176 hours on CN missions. Of those hours, 3,271 were attributed to DEA, Forest Service, local law enforcement and government agency missions. Out of these sorties, 12,090 vessels were identified, 8,266 photo recce missions were conducted, 2,643 unmarked strips were located and 340 vessels were intercepted with $2.1 million worth of property and 25,002 pounds of marijuana seized resulting in fifteen arrests. The numbers for 1991 are expected to exceed the statistics recorded for 1990.

CAP aircrews are called eyes and ears for Customs, DEA and the US Forest Service. This volunteer organization, the official USAF civilian auxiliary, assists the national counternarcotics effort with air, ground and marine reconnaissance and other missions. USAF

Wearing USAF uniforms and rank (based on time in grade), CAP aircrews donate their time, money, talents, efforts and assets to the organization's missions.

Customs-CAP Coordinators

In the heart of the Customs Air Ops West C3I facility at March AFB is an office marked Civil Air Patrol Coordinator—Bill McGrath.

Under Chuck Lampard, the National Customs CAP coordinator at CNAC, Bill McGrath is charged with coordinating all CAP activity in Air Ops West's AOR. (Both Bill McGrath and Chuck Lampard have since moved to new positions at US Customs Aviation Headquarters in Washington, D.C.)

"Not all CAP missions are generated from Customs," he explains. "Some come from a specific office of enforcement in the United States where both they and Customs become recipients of that information."

Ultimately, however, all CAP missions in the West are generated through McGrath, as those at Air Ops East are through its Customs-CAP Coordinator Russ Manhold. Most CAP tasking is initiated from a Customs unit or branch by a Customs agent. He or she may require support for reconnaissance or transportation of some sort and can request CAP involvement. "In that case," says the coordinator, "the agent has a particular reason for that plane. Not just observation or patrol or intelligence gathering, but a specific reason. Normally, I coordinate with aviation units and OE (Customs Office of Enforcement) in the West and generate missions for CAP. Missions like grid searches for possible smuggler landing strips are done every day of the week."

In 1990, CAP conducted an in-depth operation involving uncharted airstrips, code-named Operation Landmark, which was coordinated out of Customs Region Headquarters in Houston. Air Ops West supplied the mission numbers and the region was the recipient of the resulting intelligence.

"CAP provides us with excellent intelligence gathering," says McGrath. "They fly observation missions for us, they transport

Operation Border Shield requires CAP aircrews to fly continuous sorties along unmarked border boundaries *(in US airspace) over rugged, arid and mountainous terrain from Texas to California.*

114

officers, they transport evidence, they fly an average of 10,000 hours a year and we intend to expand that. In fact, this year through March 1991, the Civil Air Patrol has flown over 5,000 hours in support of Customs antidrug operations. The organization continues to get better and bigger as utilization increases.

"Take the state of Montana for instance. It is a hot spot. Why? Because 200 miles north of Great Falls are two million Canadians that are just as susceptible to cocaine as Americans are across this country."

Moreover, Customs officials believe that a cocaine transshipment pipeline, the "Canada Dry" route, exists, straight up the center of the United States, through Montana to Canada. "The Montana Wing is doing a lot of very effective intelligence gathering for us. Last year their efforts yielded $2.1 million in seized property! Oregon and Washington states are the same," he adds. "Customs utilizes CAP Wings across the nation. Oklahoma, Texas . . . we're doing a lot in those regions and are constantly conducting CAP-Customs counternarcotic orientation sessions. In fact, during the last three months, from January to March 1991, we have conducted sessions for over 700 CAP pilots and observers in Texas." And, according to the Air Ops West coordinator, "It's the same all over the West."

Orientation briefings for CAP aircrews are conducted by Customs personnel, and coordinated by Chuck Lampard and Col. Hal Bowden. As of this writing, over 5,500 CAP aircrews have received Customs orientation for counternar-

T-34s were used by CAP pilots on search and rescue and counternarcotics flights until 1990, when the vintage aircraft were ruled as being maintenance cost-prohibitive. The T-34s were phased out of CAP inventory and replaced with C-182 Skylanes that allow four crew members—a pilot, a copilot, an observer, and a scanner or law enforcement officer.

cotics operations, which makes the organization invaluable to Customs efforts in stemming the flow of illegal drugs into the United States.

Funds for CAP counternarcotic operations are approved and provided by Congress. Within congressional appropriations for the DoD in 1990, was an antidrug budget for $450 million of which $1 million was allocated to CAP. Because CAP is a volunteer organization, millions of dollars of taxpayers' money, which would otherwise be designated for the war on drugs, are saved through the dedication and professionalism of its members.

McGrath claims that, given the availability of CAP resources and the amount they are used, "CAP is undertasked! And that is not CAP's fault," he adds, "if anybody, it's Customs'. However, there's no real fault involved because we train in states like Michigan and Illinois where Customs does not use CAP resources due to very little need for aviation assets. CAP is available and it's their choice. Also, there are things the CAP cannot do. For instance, our OE would like them to be able to do specific surveillance, let's say visual air surveillance of a ground vehicle. But, they can't do that! That action is a limitation imposed by Posse Comitatus and self-imposed by Customs. The USCS cannot get the CAP in a law enforcement situation. Liability alone would be overwhelming! CAP is an auxiliary of the Air Force, basically funded by DoD money, so their involvement comes under the same [prohibited] umbrella of Posse Comitatus that restricts DoD from law enforcement action."

DoD's reconnaissance mission, under the national defense policy, is not considered law enforcement action or surveillance, and by the same token, McGrath explains, "CAP photo

Standardized USAF fleet aircraft for CAP are high-performance, fixed-gear Cessna 182s. They are equipped with state-of-the-art avionics and radios. USAF

reconnaissance missions over land or geographical areas are allowed as long as there are no action photos and no enforcement action activity! Those restrictions have affected some requests from OE only because of their misunderstanding of what Civil Air Patrol can or cannot be used for."

Not all Customs special agents attend CAP orientation briefings, although they are encouraged to participate. Those who do attend know what CAP can do and use their assets. "Like San Antonio and MacAllen," McGrath describes, "who use CAP for transportation of officers. When you deal with states like Texas, Arizona, New Mexico and some of the north central states like Montana, a Customs resident agent in charge has a staff of two agents and one intelligence analyst for a five state area! Three of his states will be border states. For him, Civil Air Patrol is a godsend! He may get a sheriff that will call and say, 'We caught this guy at the border and you might want to interview him,' but that's 800 miles away and too far for a government car to drive in one day! So, he'll get CAP to fly him and he's there in three or four hours, and back in his office that afternoon!"

Every Customs branch or unit has a resident CAP coordinator, most of whom have attended orientation briefings and make use of CAP assets. "However," McGrath admits ruefully, "there were some units who used to be [prejudiced against] CAP involvement. Having to tell those guys how well CAP was doing was like telling the Dodgers how great the Yankees were. Now that the word has gotten around, they can't wait to start using them!"

Nonetheless, there are still Customs personnel who don't care for CAP involvement, but "by and large," McGrath says, "they are criminal investigator sorts who feel threatened by *anybody* who wants to know what they are doing. It's a mindset. Basically, Civil Air Patrol only gets involved in OE missions when the Air Support Branches cannot.

"A lot of people think that because we have Citations, Cheyennes, Black Hawks, we have it all. We can't use them for a mission that a C-210 or C-182 can do because it's cost prohibitive.

The Civil Air Patrol patch.

Besides, most of the OE officers don't know the difference between a 210 and a Citation. All they need is a small airplane and that's when we call CAP."

Bill McGrath understands CAP and the aircrews who fly the missions. "My history is aviation safety, aviation training, command and control and a lot of flying hours," he remarks in reference to 2,000 flying hours in military C-130 and AC-121 crew time, 1,400 hours in Customs AWACS and 1,200 hours in other Customs aircraft (Citations, P-3s and CHETS). McGrath used to be a supervisor of detection systems on the ops floor at C3I and has worked the floor at the Albuquerque FAA Center. He took the job as CAP coordinator for Air Ops West when it was announced as a staff position and candidly admits the attractions were "a promotion and no longer having to do shift work." Although he claims to have known little about the Civil Air Patrol at the time, "I knew a lot about general aviation and intelligence gathering," he says.

"I enjoy working with CAP and have since I started. Civil Air Patrol is great! They are probably the most wondrous group of volunteers I've ever seen!"

Chapter 13

Overview and Assessment

The Customs National Aviation Center

Carol Hallet, commissioner of Customs, is the highest ranking individual in Customs. Serving directly under her authority is the Office of Aviation Operations in Washington, and Customs National Aviation Center (CNAC) field headquarters in Oklahoma. CNAC, as the backbone of the air interdiction program, is often where the buck stops.

Under Director Gerald Young and Deputy Director Joe Beaver, CNAC provides operational, administrative and logistical control accountability over all nationally deployed Customs aviation resources. It receives and disseminates all external classified and tactical intelligence related to air operations, and develops strategical plans to counter the threats by integrating C3I East and West operations, deploying AEW surveillance aircraft and responding to change in trafficking threats. Striving for 100 percent mission effectiveness with only 960 aviation personnel and 117 aircraft nationwide makes the Customs battle, against an adversary who has many more times their force and funding, unwinnable.

Flex Force

Roger Garland, former Miami branch chief now Customs Director for C3I East, has been at the front of the air interdiction battle for many years. He believes there are viable solutions to the drug problem, based on how past operations were, and present and future operations should be, conducted.

"We now get very few intruders, which means that the air program has done its job in terms of private aircraft intrusions into the US," he explains. "We've displaced them from our immediate area to land borders via tunnels, air drops and transshipments, and to ports of entry—many of which were poorly staffed—by water and commercial cargo. Illegal activity has also been displaced to the southeastern Bahamas and Puerto Rico where the majority of deliveries are air drops.

"The only way to solve this thing," Garland espouses, "is to have a complete electronic barrier in place around the entire US. Set it up and check everything that comes through the mail. And that is going to be costly, it's going to be expensive, but that's the price you're going to pay if you want to keep drugs out of America.

"The biggest problem, right now, is the southwest border," which according to Garland, "needs full-time tactical units to respond twenty-four hours a day to that threat. Our P-3s have been very effective, more so than the E-3s, plus they are cheaper to operate, more flexible, longer ranged and can get closer to the 'bowl' in terms of what's happening, and they can respond a lot quicker than the AWACS.

"We have a basic problem," he admits, "in that not everybody [who is involved in air interdiction] is reading off the same sheet of music.

We also have problems with JTF 4—a centralized command—who try to run the show. Air interdiction is unlike military operations where the guy in charge is a thousand miles away. Our philosophy in Customs is 'PIC eye ball,' meaning the pilot is in command and, he is the authority.

"Customs Air has done its mission," Garland says, "but we can't back off. Now, we have to talk deterrence. Flex force." Flex force is the flexibility to respond to varying degrees of smuggling activity with air interdiction or support interdiction between ports of entry.

"In other words," he adds, "if the threat diminished, or if that threat dried up and we knocked our law enforcement force down to 33 percent [across the board], but they come back at us within a year, Customs would be able to flex right back into a defensive posture without worrying about areas of responsibility. That's called a flex force. It's doing more with what you already have, from interdiction to alert forces, ground support work, investigations, flying between the ports of entry, finding the targets and responding with helicopters."

Bottom Lines

Drug smuggling rivals the GNP of the United States and generates billions of dollars a year for the criminal element in society who are backed by criminal organizations outside the country.

The enemy is formidable. He is smart, adaptive, crafty, immoral, unpredictable, resourceful and rich beyond most imaginations. Traffickers, unlike Customs, law enforcement and DoD warriors, do not have a fixed budget or problems with political foot dragging on procurement items. They are a capable adversary who exploit US surveillance umbrellas by applying offensive countermeasures with legal (or illegal) sophisticated, off-the-shelf, radar-calibrated detection equipment to counter existing radars, find soft spots on newer radars. They can purchase ship and aircraft schedules as easy as paying someone to deliver the goods. They monitor US home ports and airfields across the country, can monitor all communications in the

clear and intercept those that are valuable to their insidious trade.

The US low-altitude surveillance system is riddled with holes. The Aerostats help and once the fence is completed in 1992, it will cover known smuggling routes. But, what about the unknowns? And, what about the fact that it takes four Black Hawks per Aerostat (which Customs does not have) to provide sufficient strength to respond to apprehension of suspects detected by the balloons?

Airborne Early Warning P-3 Orion, E-3 AWACS, E-2C Hawkeye and AC-130 Hercules also help fill in the surveillance gaps, as do mobile ground radar sites, but there will never be enough to adequately counter the twenty-four hour a day, 365 days a year smuggling threat. Those that are available and dedicated to counternarcotics missions are personnel-intensive, high-value, high-maintenance assets subject to unpredictable down times, while their up time locations and operations are predictable to the enemy they seek.

US intelligence is developing in response to the threat and has foreseen the evolving routes in the next couple of years to be the Canada Dry routes; up both US coasts and north through the middle of the central states.

The space-based radar program must be fully implemented and the OTH-Bs are sorely needed, but their $242.8 million price tag was hard for many congressmen to justify.

The United States needs to work out the Mexico problem. Presently only the Department of State and DEA have joint working relationships with Mexico and much of that is lip service. And finally, the United States needs more long-term domestic and educational solutions.

When 1,911 arrests and 86,850 drug-related seizures valued at $23,636,219 (reported by Customs air in 1990) are considered a "drop in the bucket," it makes one wonder just what kind of a drug threat this country is up against. It also makes one wonder at the magnitude of the problem in terms of what society will face in years to come.

The fundamental principle of the National Drug Control Strategy is to make drugs undesirable and hard to get through a mix of supply and demand policies via justice, rehabilitation programs, education, international efforts aimed at drug source countries, interdiction and intelligence.

President Bush's strategy sets the American objective as 50 percent reduction within ten years in overall use of drugs. There is no quick fix say the experts but, they are only partly correct. More can be done quicker through the great American way—advertising!

Via advertising, AIDS, within two years, became a household word, its undeniable cause and effect well known to first graders and positively acted upon by junior and senior high schoolers, college students and the educated public in general.

Via millions (maybe billions?) of advertising dollars directed at antismoking campaigns, within three years millions of American smokers quit. Those who have not are made to feel and act like social outcasts.

The advertising campaigns, despite "overkill" factors, have worked, and the American public, more importantly grade-school-age children, are quite vociferous about AIDS, condoms, not putting up with smokers and "second-hand" smoke.

However, many of those same kids, who make up America's future, have no problem being in or around a group where marijuana cigarettes and other drugs are freely passed around. And those who do have a problem with it, won't "rag" or "snitch" or "tell on" others who do drugs.

In a society where it is almost easier and more sociably acceptable to snort cocaine, do crack, or light up a joint than a cigarette, it seems appropriate to suggest the following:

If the people of the United States and their elected lawmakers would get as serious about the war on drugs as they have about AIDS and getting smokers to quit, America would be light years up the road.

Aerial Smuggling and the General Aviation Public

Today's airborne illegal commodities are narcotics, automatic weapons, licensed and classified technology, software, hardware and other "small bulk, easy to ship" contraband. Smuggled items classifying as "critical technology" calling for "strategic investigation" are considered espionage and require Customs as well as FBI, CIA and NSA (National Security Agency) jurisdiction. If the smuggling involves border crossing, Customs is the enforcer and has primary jurisdiction.

Drug smuggling generates billions of dollars a year for the criminal element in society who are backed by criminal organizations outside the country. Interdiction efforts are enhanced by private pilots and the public at large who provide critical information and intelligence.

To assist in this effort, a concerned citizen can analyze the following questions pertinent to local areas:

Does the potential for aerial smuggling exist? How far is the nearest foreign border? What is the size and extent of the community and the local drug problem? How many airports are in the area? What is the extent of attempted aircraft thefts? What are the normal conditions for population, weather and law enforcement? Are low-flying aircraft the norm, or do they raise suspicions? Finally, are you a pilot or do you have access to general aviation airports? If so, you may have observed the following:

- Aircraft flying or landing after dark without lights
- Landings met by ground vehicles who quickly depart
- Load-type vehicles waiting at or near other suitable landing areas
- Pickups, trucks, vans, campers with CB equipment in those areas
- Aircraft numbers recently painted, altered or falsified
- Dried mud, no wheel fairings or pumped-up struts on landing gear
- Chipped paint or gravel marks and dents on leading edges
- Dents and scratches on underside assembly
- High-pressure fuel lines for fuel bladders
- New or nonstock exterior door locks
- Visible warps or new hinges on doors

- More than the usual number of antennae
- Badly nicked propellers
- Unusual perfume odors (to cover marijuana scents)
- Pilot requests for Mexico maps or information
- Pilot display of substantial cash
- Pilot cash payments of fuel and tiedowns
- Pilot reluctance to leave plane while being refueled
- Pilot reluctance or vagueness in answer to questions about origin or destination
- Pilot evasiveness to questions about aircraft conditions

- Aircraft parked long distances from normal observation

Additionally, if you are an FBO employee, aircraft mechanic, aviation enthusiast or in a position to casually inspect the inside of an aircraft, you may have observed the following:

- Aircraft modifications without FAA documentation
- Expensive navigation, ADF, radars or weather avionics
- Extra cockpit toggle or power switches
- Exposed fuel lines or wire harnesses in cockpit
- Internal cross braces

A smuggler aircraft flies at low altitude in an attempt to penetrate US airspace without a flight plan and without being detected.

- Internal cargo door latches
- Passenger seats removed
- Quick-connect fuel fasteners
- Torn carpets or no carpets
- Duffle bags, large trash bags, flares, fuel containers or duct tape
- Hand-operated fuel pumps, marked Mexico maps and sectionals
- Unusual perfume odors or strong air fresheners

If and when any suspicious combination of the above is observed, the public's assistance in providing that information has often been and continues to be vital to law enforcement officers and agents.

Many folks have joined the ranks of citizen warriors and received payment for their information. Under the conditions specified in 19-USCS, Section 1619, Customs is authorized to award up to $50,000 for original information leading to the recovery of fines, penalties or forfeitures for violations of Customs laws. Furthermore, any information provided to Customs concerning suspect persons or aircraft is kept in the strictest confidence when given to Customs on their national, toll free number: 1-800-BE ALERT.

Chapter 14

Fallen Warriors

Many, too many, men and women have fallen in the line of duty, service and fire during the war on drugs.

This final chapter in the story of the airborne drug hunter pays tribute to those who have lost their lives in the air interdiction mission.

"Being a warrior doesn't mean winning or even succeeding.

"It means putting your life on the line.

"It means risking and failing and risking again . . . as long as you live."

United States Coast Guard

On August 24, 1990, a Coast Guard AEW E-2C Hawkeye crashed shortly after midnight while preparing to land at NAS Roosevelt Roads in Puerto Rico.

Having been on a routine counternarcotics mission, monitoring the skies and searching for drug smugglers, the pilot reported one of the worst fears and threats to peacetime airborne aircraft, an onboard fire followed by hydraulic problems.

Onboard was a four-man crew: Lt. Duane E. Stenbak, Lt., j.g. Paul E. Perlt, Lt. Craig E. Lerner and AT1 Matthew H. Baker. All four men perished on impact.

Five days later, at Coast Guard Air Station St. Augustine, home of the crew and aircraft, a private memorial service was held where families and close friends gathered in grief. One of

the family members sent a poem to Capt. Tom Johnson, commanding officer, and requested it be shared at the service. It read:

To all my loved ones:
Do not stand at my grave and weep,
I am not there, I do not sleep.
I am a thousand winds that blow,
I am the diamond glints in the snow.
I am the sunlight on ripened grain,
I am the gentle autumn rain.
When you awaken in the morning's hush,
I am the swift, uplifting rush
Of quiet birds in circled flight,
I am the soft stars that shine at night.
Do not stand by my grave and cry,
I am not there. I did not die.

United States Customs Service

Four Customs pilots have fallen in the line of service.

On October 20, 1984, a Bell AH-1 Cobra operated by Customs was on a routine maintenance flight that ended in tragedy. Shortly after takeoff, the pilot encountered aircraft difficulties and upon flying down the airfield, the nose pitched up and the helicopter hit the ground, tail first. The aircraft was destroyed and Customs pilot Morley Miller was killed.

Three years later, on November 11, 1987, a Customs Cessna 441 crashed in mountainous terrain while on a night tactical mission. On-

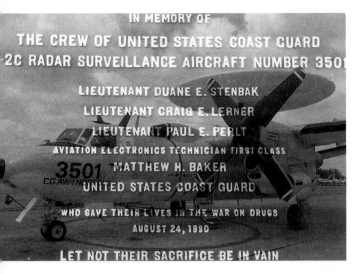

IN MEMORY OF
THE CREW OF UNITED STATES COAST GUARD
-2C RADAR SURVEILLANCE AIRCRAFT NUMBER 3501
LIEUTENANT DUANE E. STENBAK
LIEUTENANT CRAIG E. LERNER
LIEUTENANT PAUL E. PERLT
AVIATION ELECTRONICS TECHNICIAN FIRST CLASS
MATTHEW H. BAKER
UNITED STATES COAST GUARD
WHO GAVE THEIR LIVES IN THE WAR ON DRUGS
AUGUST 24, 1990
LET NOT THEIR SACRIFICE BE IN VAIN

USCG

board were Customs pilot Jim Taylor and Customs copilot Dave Crater. Both men were killed on impact.

Two years after that tragedy, the war on drugs claimed one more Customs pilot.

Miami Air Branch

March 1990 was the culmination of a twelve-month sting operation against a major trafficking ring, which netted the Miami Air Branch three tons of cocaine, $400,000 in cash and nine ringleaders. The operation, conducted with FBI agents, had been an ongoing open case where controlled narcotics deliveries to offshore vessels believed (by the traffickers) to be operating out of a warehouse in Cuba would end up in the hands of Customs agents. Customs undercover agents, believed to be bad guys, would pick up the dope and ship it to the United States where it would be stashed as evidence.

The seizure and arrest results on this bust were directly related to a controlled-delivery operation five months earlier, involving a Customs Black Hawk piloted by Ralph Gibson and George Saenz. Their bust crew were two Bahamian officers and two Customs AIOs, Joe Bendick and Chris McKinney.

Per that night-mission briefing on November 2, 1989, the weather was normal for the season: occasional thunderstorms, scattered rain showers and an overcast. The weather conditions were the kind that surface smugglers prefer when using go-fasts, high-speed, all-weather capable cigarette boats.

Customs' plan was the following:

Undercover agents posing as drug smugglers would fly north and air-drop a load of phony dope-kilos (actually plaster of Paris bricks) to real smuggler boats off the coast of Cuba (approximately fifty-five miles southeast of Marathon, Florida) in Bahamian waters. A backup Citation would "intercept and track" the "druggie" to the drop area whereupon the Hawk would swoop in and light up the boat with their night sun. The air drop was planned for 2150 hours. At the same time, prestaged US Navy hydrofoils and Coast Guard planes, helicopters and vessels would converge on the doper's position for the bust.

The smuggler's plan was to retrieve the dope and deliver it to the United States. In case of trouble they had agreed to dump the stuff overboard and run like hell for shore. The plan was known because one of the dopers was really a Customs undercover agent.

It was going to be a tough mission and as Gibson and Saenz prepared for takeoff the situational awareness was high among all crew members as they fired up the helo and took off.

Fifty-five minutes later, the smuggler aircraft has just air-dropped three floating duffel bags with light sticks to the go-fast. The Black Hawk, in place a few miles north of the doper vessel and the Cuban ADIZ, heads for the scene. Eight hundred feet above him, the AIO in the Citation confirms by FLIR that the smugglers have gaffed the "dope" onboard the boat.

The Hawk sweeps in as planned, surprising the dopers and pinning them with his night light while hovering 200 feet overhead.

The next thing the guys aboard the Hawk knew, they were in the water. It happened that fast. The crew said they felt a shudder and in a heartbeat they were underwater!

When the helo hit the water, Gibson auto-

124

matically rolled the Black Hawk right, a correct instinct bred from twenty-five years of flying that bought them precious seconds as the 12,000 pound chopper sank almost immediately! Joe Bendick, who was in the back on the left side, hit an air pocket, got some air and shot out through the gunner's window. Chris McKinney did likewise, out the opposite window, followed by the two Bahamian officers. Gibson, for whom the words *big* and *strong* are inadequate, punched the window with his fist and with total disregard to his six-foot three-inch body, forced himself through the jagged hole.

Nobody had any life support equipment other than LPUs (Life Protection Units or life vests) and none of the crew members reported looking for or finding any major door handles. They simply did not have the time. They surfaced to heavy seas and Ralph yelled for a roll call which was answered in the dark. When Saenz's name was shouted, "the crew swears that George answered the call." But, fifteen minutes later, when they were picked up, he was not there.

His death and the events surrounding that night were read into the congressional record by Congresswoman Illeana Ros-Lehtinen (R.-Florida) who knew and described Saenz as "a man of much integrity and devotion to his job who entered a Customs enforcement operation from which he never returned. George Saenz was exemplary of the American tradition that says we see a situation that is hurting the American people, their children, their families, their futures. It must be stopped. George Saenz accepted his commission with all of its risks, as Customs Service pilots do, day after day. Unfortunately, he paid the ultimate price. A massive air-sea rescue effort was launched. All possibilities were explored. The missing pilot was never found—a catastrophic result of the War on Drugs."

On February 26, 1990, a memorial service was given for George R. Saenz, US Customs Service pilot, by the Miami Air Branch to pay tribute to a fallen warrior.

Led by an honor guard, 650 people in the funeral procession attended an outdoor service at Tropical Park Law Enforcement Memorial Park in Miami.

US Customs pilot George Saenz. USCS

Branch Chief Roger Garland stood up to call the roll for the on-duty shift of November 2, 1989.

"Call the roll!" he cried.

"Attention to roll call!" replied Larry Karson, supervisor.

All the names were called, followed by responses of "Present!" until he reached George's name.

"Saenz?"

Silence.

"Saenz?"

Silence.

After a brief pause, Karson continued until all the officers names had been called.

"Sir, the roll has been called," he reported to the branch chief.

"One man missing."

Taps was played followed by a twenty-one gun salute, the traditional bagpiper and the presentation of flags to Laurie Saenz, his wife. Flanked by law enforcement honor guards and motor guards, the family and friends looked up as a formation of two Black Hawks, a Metro-Dade helicopter and an air rescue helicopter approached the park. As they came overhead, one of the Black Hawks broke off leaving a missing man formation.

Author Nena Wiley (center) poses with Miami Air Branch aircrews after participating in a mock air drop and bust performance at the 1990 Miami Air Show. Wiley is a free-lance aviation writer who has flown extensively with the airborne drug busters of the US Customs Miami Air Branch.

Index

Now from Motorbooks International, The POWER Series provides an in-depth look at the troops, weapon systems, ships, planes, machinery and missions of the world's modern military forces. From training to battle action, the top military units are detailed and illustrated with top quality color and black and white photography.

Available through book shops and specialty stores or direct. Call toll free 1-800-826-6600. From overseas 715-294-3345 or fax 715-294-4448

AIRBORNE: Assault from the Sky—
by Hans Halberstadt
America's front line parachute divisions

AIR GUARD: America's Flying Militia—
by George Hall
From the cockpit on their flying missions

ARMY AVIATION—by Hans Halberstadt
American power house; how it evolved, how it works

DESERT SHIELD: The Build-up; The Complete Story—by Robert F. Dorr
All the action leading up to Operation Desert Storm

DESERT STORM AIR WAR—
by Robert F. Dorr
Blow-by-blow account of the allied air force and naval air campaign to liberate Kuwait

DESERT STORM GROUND WAR—
by Hans Halberstadt
Soldier's-eye view of the allied ground victory over Iraq

CV: Carrier Aviation—
by Peter Garrison and George Hall
Directly from the flight deck

GREEN BERETS: Unconventional Warriors—by Hans Halberstadt
"To liberate from oppression"

ISRAEL'S ARMY—by Samuel M. Katz
Inside this elite modern fighting force

ISRAEL'S AIR FORCE
by Samuel M. Katz
Inside the world's most combat-proven air force

MARINE AIR: First to Fight—
by John Trotti and George Hall
America's most versatile assault force

NTC: A Primer of Modern Mechanized Combat—by Hans Halberstadt
The US National (Tank and Helicopter) Training Center

STRIKE: US Naval Strike Warfare Center—
by John Joss and George Hall
US Navy's "Top Gun" for ground attack pilots

TANK ATTACK: A Primer of Modern Tank Warfare—
by Steven J. Zaloga and Michael Green
American tanks and tactics in the 1990s

TOP GUN: The Navy's Fighter Weapons School—by George Hall
The best of the best

USCG: Always Ready—by Hans Halberstadt
Coast Guard search and rescue, Alaska patrol and more

SPACE SHUTTLE: The Quest Continues—
by George J. Torres
Pre-shuttle and shuttle operations history

More titles are constantly in preparation